#GOD DOESNT SUCK

#GOD DOESNT SUCK

(But Your Chronic Illness Does)

Britt D. Walker

XULON PRESS

Xulon Press
2301 Lucien Way #415
Maitland, FL 32751
407.339.4217
www.xulonpress.com

© 2020 by Britt D. Walker

All rights reserved solely by the author. The author guarantees all contents are original and do not infringe upon the legal rights of any other person or work. No part of this book may be reproduced in any form without the permission of the author. The views expressed in this book are not necessarily those of the publisher.

Unless otherwise indicated, Scripture quotations taken from the English Standard Version (ESV). Copyright © 2001 by Crossway, a publishing ministry of Good News Publishers. Used by permission. All rights reserved.

Scripture quotations taken from the Holy Bible, New International Version (NIV). Copyright © 1973, 1978, 1984, 2011 by Biblica, Inc.™ Used by permission. All rights reserved.

Scripture quotations taken from the King James Version (KJV)–*public domain.*

Scripture quotations taken from the New King James Version (NKJV). Copyright © 1982 by Thomas Nelson, Inc. Used by permission. All rights reserved.

Scripture quotations taken from The Message (MSG). Copyright © 1993, 1994, 1995, 1996, 2000, 2001, 2002. Used by permission of NavPress Publishing Group. Used by permission. All rights reserved.

(also the GNB) Scripture quotations taken from the Good News Translation (GNT). Copyright © 1992 American Bible Society. Used by permission. All rights reserved.

Printed in the United States of America.

ISBN-13: 978-1-6305-0548-6

Table of Contents

Introduction ix

Section One: Winter 1
A Brief History 3
The Grieving Cycle 11
Can We All Just Mutually Agree That This Sucks? 17
What Are the Lies Telling You? 21
You Are Enough 27
Navigating Relationships 31
Do I Really Want God? 37
New Memories 41
Rethinking the Whale 45

Section Two: Spring 51
Enapay 53
What Are You Walking Out of Egypt With? 57
Self-Care 61
All the Things 67
When Life Goes On 77
What Do I Write? 83
Who You Are 87
What's Your Iceberg? 91

On Dens and Fire 93
Oh, That Healing 97
And Only Sometimes Let Your Conscience Be Your Guide 101
Be a Betsy 103
Why Not Me? 109
The Source of It All 113

Section Three: Summer 119
Let's Go Back to Fear 121
The Two Ways 127
Anger 129
Promises of Strength 133
Re-Learning Trust 137
You Are Not Sick Girl 141

Section Four: Autumn 147
The Cure 149
You Can Handle This 153
Condemnation 155
God's Turn: "If You Only Really Knew" 159
A Year Called Growth 161
But How Do I Really? 165
The Second Half 169
Even Better Than Before 173
At Least Remember This 177

References 179

Dedication:

To Abba, Jesus and the Holy Spirit. You gave me the words before I even believed they were true. This is for you.

To my best friend and baby daddy of our kids. I still love you in my life.

To McCrae and Paxton, you are my miracles. Redemption in physical form. You are loved more than you will ever know.

Introduction

"It's just stress." How many of us started our health journey with this statement? It makes sense, though. That's why we fall prey to its allure. It's just the season of life we are in with our job, partner, relationships, parents, baby, toddler, teenager, [fill in the blank]. It's just stress. But for some, that season of stress didn't end. We never shook the feelings in or from our mind and body, and we began to worry.

If this is you, let me first start by saying, "Hi," and that sucks. I wish you did not ever have to read this book. That may be weird for an author to write, but it's 100 percent true. I wish chronic illness was just an optional diagnosis on your WebMD search, which ultimately turned out to be a paper cut. No, this is not what you had in mind when you envisioned your life, but you need to know this: It's not the end. This is just an open invitation to start over and even do it better if you let it.

I guess in a book about chronic illness, you jump right in. There is no plot twist like, and then she got sick, and everyone is like, "NOOO." It would be even weirder if I were just writing this book about what I *think* it may feel like to be diagnosed with a chronic illness. That is just brazy (brazen and crazy). I wrote this book for a few reasons. First, because I felt like God was telling me to. Yep, the Big Man. I am not an "open book" (pun intended) kind of a girl. I don't really like people to know my deep struggles, so writing about them for, let's be honest, my family and the friends they bribed to read it, was not my first impression of a fun time. But my ego got a jump on me, and I started envisioning a book with my picture on the back cover and first-class plane trips to speak at conferences with my new besties, Beth Moore and Rachel Hollis. Yep, I go big or go home. But as I wrote this book, I realized I wrote it for me: for my heart. So I could make sense of this all. So I could understand all the gobbledy-goop in my brain. So I could read the truth. Having a chronic illness can suck, but it is even suckier when you blame God for it, or cannot understand the nature of God in spite of it. I wrote this book because I needed so many answers when I got diagnosed, and I mostly got the sympathetic head nods of not-sick people telling me, "Everything happens for a reason." I am glad to say I never once throat-punched a person for saying that. I am basically a saint.

I often found myself wandering in the dark, trying to find my way out, by myself, while sick and anxious. Super fun way to travel! I needed a guide. I needed someone to tell me the truth and then tell it to me again and again. I needed to hold on to it physically. So here it is. That thing. The truth, written in a book about what I have learned on this journey so far. I wrote it in small sections because, let's be honest, brain fog is real, and when I need to grasp a principle to heart, I can only take small doses. Also, this book is geared toward women. Men are absolutely permitted and encouraged to read this book, the principles and truths are not gender-specific, but of the 26 million Americans living and coping with an autoimmune disease, more than seventy-five percent of them are women.[1] Plus, I am a woman, so I get the struggle on a personal level. Also, you will get an extra helping of sarcasm, because it's basically my love language.

This book is my year-long journey to finding truths amid so many lies. My hope for this book is that it helps ease your mind. I desperately pray it will bring health to your bones. But most of

Introduction

all, I hope this brings you closer to the one person who is so <u>brazy</u> about you: God. May you find all you need in Him.

Your fellow sojourner and friend:

Britt

Section One
Winter

A Brief History

I was diagnosed with Hashimoto's disease on August 3, 2016, an autoimmune disorder that destroys your thyroid gland, which is a butterfly-shaped organ that lives in your neck. Up until that point, I am not even sure I could tell you where the thyroid was located in the body. What functions does it control, you ask? The answer is apparently EVERYTHING. Every little thing that makes the body function well, such as heart rate, metabolism, emotions, organ function, just to name a few. My brand of Hashimoto's was an overachiever, which is truly no surprise given that I am, in my words, "a recovering perfectionist." It basically said, "If we are going to die, we are going out guns a-blazing." And so, it dramatically started releasing all of its stored hormones into my body all…at…once. If you need a mental image, it's basically like shoving your finger into a light socket while drinking a gallon of Red Bull. It changed everything in my life.

I had to quit my job, move in with my parents for support, and hire a nanny to help me care for my infant daughter. For seven months, I dramatically lost weight, had body tremors, my heart rate never went below 100 beats per minute, and I panicked. Dear Lord, the panic. It both figuratively and literally brought me to my knees. I was raised in a Christian home but had become calloused to God after walking through infertility. But I knew I would not get through this without divine intervention.

If you struggle with this disease, I am sure you also know the fun time of trying out different medications and dosages to see which works for you. My first try was a disaster, which resulted in my body overreacting to the medicine. My body shook so bad I legitimately had a tongue tremor. During that episode, I remember sitting on my in-laws' front porch, shaking and looking up to the sky. "God, I don't know what to do. Please speak to me. Say anything." That's when I heard it, "I will heal you." I mean, of course, that is what I wanted to hear from God. How lucky was I that the God of the universe was going to give me a miracle!?! But of course that is not what He said. God said, "I will heal you," and I, in turn, expected a miraculous healing of my thyroid. I asked a pastor friend of mine to pray on my behalf to see if God would confirm this message to her as well. Since she is a pastor, I figured she should be tight with God. She graciously agreed. Then I politely asked her about the weather for days and, "Oh, have you heard anything from God? Asking for a friend…" After a few days, she gave me this verse: "For your wounds, I will heal and your health I will restore" (Jeremiah 30:17). "God would heal me," she confirmed.

So when the hell in my body did not cease, you can imagine my dismay. Seeing that this course was not very sustainable, my endocrinologist recommended I have my thyroid removed. But I was so determined to force the hand of God into the miracle He "promised," I was having none of it. My family finally had to stage an intervention, and I pridefully stated that if God would open the doors to surgery, I would then walk through them. This would show them to trust God. Well, those doors flew wide open. And so I tentatively walked through them.

One of the risks of thyroid removal is voice loss. I was assured by my doctor this would not happen to me since I was slender, and there is only an overall two percent chance of this occurring. With this reassurance, I agreed to the surgery.

The night before the surgery, I sat on my in-laws' front porch and taped a video message to my daughter, just in case things did not go according to plan. I wanted her to always be able to hear me say, "I love you," even if I could no longer speak. But I knew it was going to be okay. They were going to open me up and find a perfectly healed thyroid, and it was going to be a miracle. On the off chance this did not happen, if God wanted me to have this surgery, He would never allow me to lose my voice, right? Oh, the sweet naiveté. So I had my surgery, and then I lived happily ever after. The End. Oh, do I wish, but this would be a very short and pretty pointless book if that is where this journey ended. Instead, the surgeon found my thyroid in such bad shape that it was difficult to remove.

After surgery, my voice did not recover as planned. My surgeon said he thought I was just straining my voice and needed to stop talking so much. I would have what I called "silent days" where I would use my own version of sign language to communicate and write on a small whiteboard I carried around with me. I will never forget the terror I felt when my dog got loose and ran into the street, and I tried to scream for him to stop, and nothing came out. I felt out of control and small. My internal dialogue sounded something like this: "What the crappola is this? You promised to heal me, and then You didn't, then You allowed me to lose my voice????" It took three months of straight-up denial and sounding like a sexy, smoking grandma before my husband said I needed to go see an Ears Nose and Throat ("ENT") doctor. I begrudgingly made an appointment. But I knew nothing was wrong, I just needed to be quiet more often, and it would all be okay. The ENT was quick with the draw to push the tube through my nose and down my throat. I sat, grasping the sides of the chair. He apologized as he removed the device. I thought he meant for shoving the thing down my throat without warning. But he repeated his sympathy as he stated, "I'm sorry, your right vocal cord is paralyzed. You are probably going to want to consult with a malpractice attorney." I should have, but did not see this coming. I mean at all. I welled up with tears, ended the consultation, and walked out. How could God allow this to happen if this had been His will?

To break the suspense, I will at least inform you that this portion has a happy ending. I know the prayers of many were heard when weeks later I went to pick up my little girl from her crib and said, "Good morning, baby." My voice sounded a bit stronger, and it grew from there. Never fully reaching its former state of strength, but certainly a miracle nonetheless.

In the year that followed, I began to have severe stomach pains and would have to have "smoothie only days" because I could not swallow well. I developed muscle spasms in my chest and stomach. I had severe tension headaches that caused tremendous pain and dizziness. I saw seventeen specialists and underwent multiple procedures. We finally consulted with the Mayo Clinic, just hoping to find any relief and answers. My anxiety was through the roof. The excellent Rheumatologist at the Mayo Clinic was the sweetest doctor I had ever met. He embodied the feeling and look of Santa Claus, and he patiently told me I had Centralized Sensitization Syndrome. A catch-all diagnosis that basically means your Central Nervous System is keeping you in fight or flight mode, but there is no pinpoint origin as to why. So we finally had a name, but no cure. He gave me a pamphlet on stress management and a "Go with God" nod, and that was that.

Narrator: "But she did not go with God."

No. I went with control and stress-out city. Since my entire endocrine system was somewhat of a crap show, my docs decided to check out my pituitary. And as the story of my life would go, I went for the MRI. By "went for my MRI," I mean I panicked and focus-breathed through the whole thing, but then felt relief once done because there was no way I had a brain tumor (you think I would have learned by now). When they asked me to come back for more imaging, I wavered a bit, but kept up that good ole denial brain. My doctor personally called me the next day. Folks, that is never, and I mean never, a good sign. They are never like, "Hey, you won a million dollars." It's more like, "Hey, sorry, but you have a brain tumor." My local endocrinologist and the Mayo Clinic Endocrinology Department could not agree on what the next step should look like, and I basically spent the month of December 2018 in a hyper-state of panic. I had not seen my life going this way.

In desperation, we are willing to do a lot of things we would not otherwise feel the need to resort to. Fear was the only thing I could see. I was terrified of the future and was really meditating on my own humanity. I even told my husband to pick a new wife who would love our daughter if something were to happen to me. I felt hopeless.

But God…you have to love a "but God" moment. I will never forget it. I stood in my kitchen, trembling with adrenaline and anxiety. I had reached my enough. I was sick of being the weak, broken down, punching bag of fear. I was sick of wasting my every bloody second of mind space on terror scenarios. I was sick of fearing what I could not control. I was sick of feeling helpless against the onslaught of thoughts and internal feelings. I had had enough. So I paced in my kitchen like a lion in a cage. I screamed at the top of my lungs: "You have messed with the wrong girl. I am done. I am done. I am done. You do not own me fear. I am not your slave. You are not my master. I may have to walk through this, but I do not have to fear this. Get out." My husband thought I had lost my ever-loving mind. But actually, this is when I began to find it. This was my breaking and reckoning, my "breakoning." I would never be the same after this moment.

Don't misunderstand. I was not miraculously healed. Neither did I stop experiencing fear and anxiety. The thing that changed that day was, for the first time, I chose to believe God for who He said He was and for what He said He would do. I chose to believe

He had not given me a spirit of fear, but a spirit of Power and Love and a Sound Mind (2 Timothy 1:7 NIV). I chose to believe this state of being was not His desire and plan for me (Jeremiah 29:11 NIV). I chose to believe He had a vested interest in my life. I chose to believe He loved me (John 3:16 NIV). I chose to believe I was not a victim of my circumstances. I chose to believe I had everything I needed within me to succeed and that greater is He that is in me than he that is in the world (1 John 4:4 NIV). I chose to believe Satan is just a liar and an illusionist and had no power to control my thoughts (John 8:44 NIV).

I wrote these truths on my mirror, arms, index cards I placed in my car, on the home screen of my phone, over multiple journals, and notes on my cellphone. I repeated them over and over again. The mantra: "I don't have to feel this, I just have to believe this," was spoken over and over again. Until one day, it began to feel like the truth.

You may be engaged in a similar story, and you know this in no way is the easy road. So let me help you unload some lies you may be carrying around.

> *You are not doing this to yourself.* There you go. Badge of guilt removed from your chest.
>
> Here are some other truths you may need to hear:
>
> *This is not your fault.*
>
> *Your body does not hate you.*
>
> *You are not less than now.*
>
> *You are not damaged goods.*
>
> *You are not ruining your family's life.*
>
> *You're not a bad mother because you have a particular diagnosis.*
>
> *You are not a bad wife.*
>
> *You are not a victim.*
>
> *You are not weak.*

We did not cause this, but there are some things we may allow to dwell in our hearts and minds that are not true that may make this harder for ourselves. "It is for freedom that Jesus set us free" (Galatians 5:1 NIV). You and I are free. Now let's start acting like it.

The Grieving Cycle

Why does God allow bad things to happen to good people? It's an age-old question and the answer for me is ever-evolving. When I was first diagnosed, I could barely care for myself. The medications to heal and help were not so much doing their jobs. Although, in retrospect, I think a lot of the feelings and sensations throughout my body could have been the direct result of the thoughts I allowed to free-float in my mind unbridled. I felt like a victim of my circumstances, and victim mentality will never lead to wholeness. Nonetheless, it is still a journey we must walk through so the pain of remaining stuck drives us to change. Or maybe that is just me; perhaps you are entirely wise and can look at others and not fall into their snares. My preference is trial by fire. Or at least it was.

I cried so much for myself in those beginning years. I was so self-focused on how this made me feel. How in the world was I going to be "something?" I am an Achiever on the Enneagram for heaven's sake! I sat in it, and let me tell you why it's okay to do that. Here is your permission card. The God of the universe created emotions. So before Dr. Elisabeth Kubler-Ross ever penned the Stages of Grief (denial, anger, bargaining, sadness, acceptance), God had already created the cycle. He did this for us. God knew we would need the denial at the beginning so we could take care of the initial work that needs to be done when we are hit with overwhelming grief, such as planning for the unknown future and making the next appointments.

He knew we would get angry and question. And if you are a Christian for longer than one hour, you tend to direct that anger in His direction. "Why would you?" we spit out with vehement rage. Guess what? God is a big boy, and He can handle it. Also, and I'm not sure any Christian is genuinely aware of this, but we do not have to answer for God; there, I said it. We can let Him speak for Himself to the heart of the one that is hurting, and we can legitimately sit there next to her, holding her hand in silence. ::Bomb drop:: No, I am serious; this is an option. It's the best option. It is not a requirement that we tell someone hurting that "God has a plan for everything" and "I will pray for you" and then not. I love that Judaism has "sitting in shiva," meaning to sit and mourn with those who mourn. There is a time for that. Ecclesiastes 3:4 (NIV) says it clearly: "there is a time to weep, a time to laugh, a time to mourn, a time to dance." We do well to let the season be, and walk through it, instead of trying to drag someone or ourselves through each step before its time.

The bargaining is next, and this is where I got stuck for a bit, and to be honest, it's where the hottest, ugliest tears come from. What about my family, God? Fine, I accept this is happening to me. I will let down my martyrdom. I will choose to believe You love me. I will choose to believe this is for my good. I will choose to believe You will give me a future so full of hope it will rock my socks off. I will choose to believe You delight in mercy and not judgment, and this is not a punishment. I will choose to believe this will bring me closer to my most authentic self; the self you created me to be; the one I have always wanted to be, but was too scared, too ill-equipped, too insecure about becoming without Your divine help. I will choose to believe the divine is within me, and I have everything I need to succeed. I will believe I can do this…every flare-up, every pain, every restless night, every emotion because You give me strength.

But what about them? My husband didn't sign up for this when we said our vows a decade ago. Oh sure, he said "in sickness and in health." But I think we were both counting on the "in health" part or, in the very least, that health will return. The woman he married is not the woman he is still married too. I watch him struggle with his own thoughts and emotions in every wave of a flare-up, I have watched him grow angry at You, God, and shake his head in disbelief that this is his life too. I have felt him grow distant when he could not process this new normal. I have seen the look of lost expectations in his eye. That look that says, "I just did not see my life turning out this way." Why wouldn't You change this for him because You love him? Why wouldn't You perform a miracle in my life to strengthen his faith? Or better yet, why would You allow my precious daughter, the one You handpicked for me to parent, watch her mother be sick? I prayed so desperately for her when we were going through infertility, and now I am a sick mom??? I want to run around the yard with her. I want to play non-stop. I want to be patient and kind, and being sick has a funny way of bringing out the worst side of me at times. I want to say I love you more than I am sorry. So the bargaining starts. Heal me for their sakes. Heal me so I can be a better mom and wife. Heal me so I can do more for them and You. But then God gently reminds me: "I love family. I love marriage. I love children. And I love your family more than you love them. I have a plan for them in this, as well. I did not leave their lives to chance. I will give them all the tools I am providing you. Give them to me. You never had control over their lives anyway."

Sadness comes trolling in next. I remember the time I was sitting in my counselor's office telling him "I just feel so sad." He gently reminded me of the stages of grief. "The sadness stage sucks the most. But you are almost at the end." For some reason, that was comforting. The acknowledgment that this sadness was okay. That I would be okay. That this is normal. You must mourn the life you *had* before you can accept the life you *have*. This does not mean the life you had before was better, and now life from here on out sucks or is subpar at best. That is a crock of crap. All this means is that the old must be relinquished in order for you to get to the new: acceptance.

I found my way to acceptance in Disney. Mind you, this introvert does not think the "happiest place on earth" is all that great. The crowds, the heat, the crowds. Yikes. But my daughter was four years old at the time, and she had not seen the movie *Up*,[2] so my husband and I decided to have a fun family cuddle time and introduce her. If you haven't seen *Up*, spoiler alert: The film starts with a tomboy little girl and a cautious little boy who grow up together and get married. They are lying on a hilltop one day and are looking at the clouds, pointing out things they see when all of the clouds start to look like babies to them. So they try to have a baby. But they can't. They show the man and woman in the office of their fertility doctor as the man sits stalwart, and the woman cries into her hands. Later the woman passes away, and the man thinks he has lost his greatest adventure, so he ties a ton of balloons onto their house, and it floats away to his dream, only for him to realize the destination is not the dream, but the journey. So my husband and I sat on our bed with our four-year-old daughter in between us and we cried like babies. We had not made a note in our brains to remember this scene. The sweet young things that we were when we got married and first saw this movie, never thought we would ever deal with something like infertility. When we were young and naïve, we lost sleep over trying to prevent pregnancy as if we had the only say.

Up brought up (I like my puns intended) so many things. Infertility, the loss of our perceived dreams and destinations, the loss of a life that once was. All lost expectations. The expectation of what was must always be released to allow the new to be born. But that cannot just be done. It is a breakoning; at least in my case. I had to break open, pour my sobbing heart out to God with my hands open and say, "These are my precious things, my hopes and dreams. Will you treat them kindly? Will You love them as I have loved them? Will You really promise me that if I give them to You, Your dreams will actually be better? Will You make this hurt a little less?"

The Grieving Cycle

I prayed, and if you think about doing this, don't skip this step. The devil wants nothing more than to drown you in your perceived failures and disappointments. You are opening Pandora's box, there is a lot of emotion behind this. Don't give him a foothold. I literally prayed, "Satan, I command you and all your minions to be bound and gagged along with your backups, replacements, weapons, claims, and devices, and be sent to the throne room of God for your punishment. You have no place here." Is that too Pentecostal for you? Good! Know your authority, Girl. Speak it out. You can say it with trembling hands and quivering lips, but by golly say it, and BELIEVE it. All Satan has is lies and illusions. Stop giving him power that he does not have. Stop believing what Satan cannot do and start believing what God can do. Then sit down and write out all of your expectations. Cry until you have no more tears. Then gently roll up those pieces of paper, put them in a balloon, and let it go. Literally. Let it all go. Pray again as you watch it fly to the heavens, as you hear your spirit softly whisper, "Behold, don't you see it, I am doing a new thing" (Isaiah 43:19). This is how you get to the final stage of acceptance. Give it to God. Let your expectations go and embrace the future God has planned for you. You have to open your hands and let the balloon fly away. It will be worth it.

Hear this if you hear nothing else: God will not smite you, hurt you, or be angry with you for going through any of the stages of grief. I don't care if you say all the big boy language in the world at Him. He knows pain sucks. Remember, Jesus had a physiological response to stress by sweating drops of blood. Jesus cried. Jesus felt abandoned by God. Jesus couldn't carry His own cross. You are doing the best that you can, and God loves you.

Can We All Just Mutually Agree That This Sucks?

I was sitting on the floor in my devotion spot (for me, it needs to be soft and well-lit with natural light. None of this artificial nonsense. Just me, bare feet, and Jesus. If a cup of tea and a cozy sweater happens to join, all the better). My love decided to lay next to me on the floor when I blurted out, "Do you think there will ever be a time where we can just say this frackin' sucks, put our middle fingers in the air, and just let it be?"

He sat up and said, "Yeah, babe, I think one day we can." I know I tend to self-sabotage. I feel the flare-up meandering its way through my body and I think, "Oh shiitake, how am I going to handle this one? Be cool, Brittany, maybe it won't see you." But what if we changed the script? What if this time we weren't a victim of our circumstances and body, but a warrior? What if we said, "Bring it." Let's determine the narrative beforehand.

Ummm, also, as a side note, if you are a "grasp the pearls" kind of person at the mention or suggestion of swear words, this may not be the book for you. Brene Brown, Ph.D., LMSW, and Christian says it perfectly: "I can confidently say that stories of pain and courage almost always include two things: praying and cussing. Sometimes at the exact same time."[3] I try my best to keep it clean, but sometimes guys, I am not perfect. And if you are looking to read a book written by a perfect person, Mother Teresa has a lovely book called *No Greater Love*.

The next time you feel the wave-a-coming, agree with your mind that this sucks, and then say, "I will do what I can, when I can, however I can, with as much grace as I can, to wash over it all. It is still good. This is enough." Did you need to get take-out because you were too exhausted to cook? Awesome. I love Chipotle; order me a bowl. Did brain fog make you forget the laundry in the washer too long and then you had to rewash it and then forgot it again? No worries. Those stinky socks probably needed an extra scrubbing. Did you snap at your child because they were obnoxious, and you could not hear "Let it Go" one…more…time? Amazing! Teaching your children everyone makes mistakes and has to apologize is a valuable lesson. Did you lose it with your spouse, who is sitting on the sofa, utterly oblivious to the mess and your current mental state? Well, welcome to marriage. He is a big boy, and a head rub later should do the trick.

And guess what? The above list of transgressions is made, *on the daily*, by fully healthy moms and wives. This is not mutually exclusive to those whose bodies decide they want to be real jerks sometimes. This is what it means to be human and grow. Darling, you are going through more on any given day than the average mama bear. Remember that. You deal with the daily stressors of life, disappointments, losses, and struggles, but you also do all this with a chronic illness. Any of the above stresses people to their max, and you are already operating in the negative. This is not to upset you. This is to infuse a little truth into your situation. I often will get frustrated with myself for not handling a situation better. Or will browbeat myself for not immediately turning to compassion when hit with some annoyance in my family. I want to be better; do better. But it is in these moments I am losing sight of the facts and grace. As it's a typical symptom of chronic illness, I don't think it's a stretch to say most of us struggle at least on and off with sleep disturbance. Most of us have flare-ups. Most of us experience a sense of pain and discomfort on a chronic basis. Most of us are not at a Kardashian level with stylists, daily maids, and full-time chefs. The simple fact you are reading this book permits me to imply that most of us have struggled with our emotions through this process. All of this needs an ample covering of grace.

Give yourself so much margin for error. Bathe yourself in mercy and grace. Learn to forgive yourself because a "person who is forgiven much shows great love" (Luke 7:47 NIV). It is possible to admit that this sucks and not wallow. There is a massive difference, and your mental and physical health rests on you dividing these two things. You don't have to lie. You don't have to pretend. If anything, that may do more damage to you. Speaking truth out loud is often the most freeing thing in the world. It's like lifting the lid on a boiling pot, so it does not spillover. As Shauna Niequist says in *Present Over Perfect*, "Pour out the vinegar to God so you can get to the rich oil below."[4] But you cannot stop there. Hear me. YOU CANNOT END THE CONVERSATION THERE. You must then tell yourself the truth. "This sucks, but I can do all of this because He gives me strength (Philippians 4:13 NIV). This sucks, but my husband is still standing beside me, and he has a choice; thank you, God, he is choosing to be here. This sucks, but my baby girl brings me so much joy. This sucks, but [fill in your blank]."

Love yourself as you are, completely flawed with or without an autoimmune condition. Confidence is the sexiest feature you have. So walk in it. This flare-up is not your life. This disease is not your name. This season is not your eternity. Know this. Tattoo this on your body if you need to. Have the swagger of a woman who knows she can look hell straight in the face and know it ain't got nothing on her. Not today, Satan! This may suck. You may get a few kicks in the pants, but do not gloat over me, enemy! Though I may have fallen, I will rise. Though I sit in darkness, the Lord will be my light (Micah 7:8).

What Are the Lies Telling You?

It's a question I try to ask my inner spirit daily. What are the lies telling you? Satan is the author of lies and an illusionist. He has no power in himself, but only what we allow him to have in our lives. His favorite tool is lies. It feeds all other toxicities in our bodies. I often fall prey to fear. The unknown, the what if, the how can. It's all lies. But often, I have taken these lies and made them truth in my subconscious. Thus, the neural pathways have become superhighways built with bricks of lies. Take writing this book, for instance. The lies sounded like this:

Lies:

1. You are a fraud.
2. You have nothing to say.
3. You won't say it well.
4. It's already been said.
5. You are too prideful to write a book.
6. You don't have the credentials to write a book about God.
7. You aren't passionate enough to complete this project.
8. You are too consumed by your own thoughts and emotions to do anything else.
9. You will be lonely and isolated.
10. You are not enough.
11. If you write this, you will be heavily attacked by Satan, and you will fail.

Ladies, this crap is relentless. But it is first and foremost, crap, full-on donkey doo-doo. But we will keep etching deeper neural pathways with this hogwash because we don't know how to reverse it. This was me for years. I am such a nerd for systems. I love order, and I am pretty sure Marie Kondo and I would be BFF's. So if there needs to be a five-point system created to guarantee success in X-Y-Z, this girl is going to find it or create it. I am not doing it out of pride, honestly. I just think I am responsible for fixing myself. It goes like this: I will have a stroke of genius (which is really an eye-opening from the Holy Spirit) as to Satan's game and the lies, and then I immediately say, "Thank you, God, I have it from here. I will claim my authority and then create a system that will create life-long change. You're welcome." I usually start by changing my background picture to something inspirational. Then I write copious notes in my phone of things I need to change. Then the planning. Oh, the planning. I will wake up at this time, write in my gratitude journal, read 2.5 small devotions on the Bible App, then pray in the shower, I will write pen notes on my hand to keep a reminder of what I need to change, I will get internally judgy at my husband for his inability to change, I will do another devotional in the afternoon, I will only listen to Christian Music, nay, praise music by Bethel, because that stuff is jam-packed with Jesus ju-ju. Then I usually drop from exhaustion and perfectionism. Because who the heck can keep that up?! I have a four-year-old for crying out loud. And yet I do it, time after time after time. Because I fail to remember God is the only one who can truly achieve the lasting change my heart needs. God is the one knocking at the door of my heart to show me, "Hey darling, something needs to change here, because it's better for you in the long run and because I love you. And guess what? If you let me, I will even do it for you. You don't have to work yourself into exhaustion."

God has a vested interest in our lives, in our changing. We are His hands and feet. We are His representation to the world of who He is and how He acts. Don't you think He is invested in how that looks in what we say and do and how that all plays out to your family member who is going through a divorce? To your co-worker who lost a child? To your LGBTQ neighbor? He is not looking for exhausted soldiers. Nor is He looking to exhaust His soldiers. He literally says, "for my yoke is easy, and my burden is light" (Matthew 11:30 NIV). He wants to unburden us. He wants to help us. He wants to change our hearts. He wants us to rest in Him, in His power, in His strength. We do not have to get to the end of our ropes before He permits us to call on His name. No, that is what striving has told us. That is what conditional love requires of us. This quid pro quo world says we have to give in order to get. But that is not true of God. He does not play by our man-made rules. He says, "You can never out-give me. You can never out-love me. You can never earn this. And that is exactly how I intended it. You want to know why? Because I love you. Love the snot out of you." You are esteemed and honored in my sight (Isaiah 43:8 NIV).

It's the old adage, *physician heal thyself*. You don't take advice well from a sick physician. And the world is not going to listen to exhausted Christians who are killing themselves to perform. God will lead you "beside still waters" (Psalms 23:2). He will refresh your soul.

So about those lies from the beginning. They cannot be permitted to stay. The truth must also be said. New neural pathways of life created. You must write a truth for every lie.

Truths:

1. I believe every word I wrote in this book about God. His strength, love, mercy, and compassion. I do not always use the tools correctly, but that is because I am a human being. This is a part of my battle. This human struggle does not negate my voice or these truths.

2. I have a push from God to speak out the truth of His love. I know I am passionate about this. Speaking God's love and truth to an audience of one or millions is still worth it.
3. God will work within me to give me the message, and a brilliant editor should hopefully help with the rest. I do not have to be an expert on writing to write.
4. Yes, there is nothing new under the sun. The truths of God and His love are not new things, and yet people do not grasp them or understand them until it is their time to. I may be adding a book to the thousands on this topic, but people still need to hear the truth, and so it needs to continue to be said.
5. Yes, pride can be an issue, but a humble heart that gives this fear to God will see victory and freedom.
6. I can study. Jesus used fishermen to spread His message, not the religious leaders of the day. He can use me and teach me.
7. God will restore my passion and give me vision. I declare this in Jesus' name.
8. God has given me a strong mind, and a spirit of love and joy and peace and longsuffering, gentleness, goodness, faith, meekness, and temperance. I will watch His mighty hand. He is making a way in the wilderness. He is doing a new thing in my life. He is breaking chains. I lay it all down at His feet. It is too much for me to carry on my own.
9. This is a time to learn, to be quiet, to write, but also to explore and be flexible. God has also given me this gift. Lord, give me the heart and strength to use it.
10. I am enough. Right now. As I am. Always.
11. If I do not write this, I will still be attacked. This book should help gird me to deeper levels of trust and love of God.

So what are your lies telling you? What are those destructive feelings and thoughts you just can't shake? What are the things you have come to believe about yourself that make you feel *less than*? Say them out loud, write them down. Then call them what they are: lies. But never, ever end with the lies. You must go to your truth. To do that, you must know your truths. Study God's word. Google God's promises. Read books on God's love and character. Talk to Him. This is how you get to the truth. It is the foundation of every good thing from God and every defense against the enemy. The more you fill your mind with the truth, the better you will feel, both mentally and physically. The lies will only allow you to see this disease as sickness. The truth will reveal this as a time of rebranding and rebirth. The lies will viciously judge you by your pre-diagnosis standards. The truth will set you free from unrealistic standards and better priorities. The lies will load you with guilt. The truth will allow you to walk with more genuineness and compassion than you ever imagined. The truth will set you free.

You Are Enough

I have only been smitten by one personality type test: the Enneagram. It has risen in popularity over the years. If you are unfamiliar, I definitely think you will find it personally helpful and a good use of phone surfing while you are waiting for an appointment. I am a three on the Enneagram, which equals the Achiever. "People of this personality type need to be validated to feel worthy; they pursue success and want to be admired. They are frequently hard-working, competitive, and are highly focused on the pursuit of their goals. They are often 'self-made' and usually find some area in which they can excel and thus find the external approbation which they so desperately need."[5] Fun, right? Basically, I was born with a complex that likes to yell very loudly, "You are not enough; you must do more."

My parents were first-generation Christians and were doing the best they could in leading our family to Christian churches and schools. Unfortunately, those institutions were terribly unbalanced and not anywhere close to what and who Christ is. They stunk of condemnation, and the love of Christ was washed away in the blood of guilt. "You must act like this. You must dress like this. You must say these things. You may not go there or here. You may not go outside of these confines, and you may never, ever question these rules." Did I mention I am a rule follower? Give me a set of guidelines, and I am like, "Hot dog, I got this!" I have zero confusion as to where the perfectionism came from that controlled my life for years. This was a perfect storm. I remember being so scared to make a mistake because not only would those in authority be disappointed, but God would hate me until I did penance with a thousand good acts, and then maybe He would consider allowing me back into heaven. Yikes. My heart grieves for this child who would sit on her bed scared of hell, thinking she deserved it because she spit out some of her vegetables in her napkin.

I preached the love of God like it was some magical unicorn. It may exist, but no one has ever seen it. At least I had never seen it. I kid you not, I used to pray that God would physically hurt me if I went to sin. I cannot imagine how this must have hurt the heart of God. If my daughter ever came up to me and said, "Mom, I want you to take this taser and zap me every time you see me about to do something I shouldn't," I would be very, very concerned. With this mess of toxic Christianity, my mind said there was no way I was going to make it to heaven or my calling. I was used up by the time I was in my twenties.

At a local favorite vintage shop (I love interior design, and a Saturday fifty percent off estate sale is my jam), I saw the following quote from Lisa Bever on a sign that changed my life: "If you think you've blown God's plan for your life, rest in this: you, my beautiful friend, are not that powerful." Y'all, I started crying big wet tears. The antiques can verify the story. I felt broke open.

Here's the thing: I am not sure I was aware, but I am not more powerful than the Creator of the entire universe, and if that quote was correct, He still saw value in me, and He was saying, "I can still use all of this." I could not fathom why He would want to. The problem is that I did not know whose I was. In my mind, I was alone. I had to do it all on my own. I had to earn. I had to strive. I would be graded harshly and not on a curve. I was a lousy sinner who did not deserve mercy because I did this to myself.

This statement ruminated in my mind for two years. I just could not get the feeling to stick, to go from my head to my heart. Flare-ups would come, and I would fall apart. The guilt I took into my heart was overwhelming. I felt like this illness was a punishment, and if I were stronger or better, I would not keep having these awful symptoms. If I were a better Christian, God would stop this. I especially believed the lies I saw written on my husband's face that said, "I have had enough. You are not worth this." I let guilt determine the narrative, and then I drowned in my own self-pity.

Well, that jerk-off inner critic was half right. I could never earn my mercy because I did not have to. I was a sinner. There was a record, but there was no information written after my name because it had all been wiped clean. I am a child of the most-high God and He has great plans for my life. I am so very loved and held and seen and given everything I need and then some. I am doted on by angels who protect me. I am surrounded by the God of the Angel Armies who fights my battles and counts it as victory for me. He wants to do awesome, amazing, miraculous stuff for me and through me, and not just once in a lifetime. But daily, and I mean daily. He wants to hear all the vinegar and all the fine wine of my day. He wants me to yell at Him when I don't understand because the pain is so deep, and He will gently answer to comfort my heart. He sends signs and friends and strangers to confirm His love and word to comfort my questioning heart. I am worth this to Him. I am enough for Him.

So I started this mantra: "I am enough. As I am. Right now. Always." I would say it when the flare-ups would come, and I would start the striving all over again to make up for the guilt. I would say it every time my husband would resort to silence because he did not know what to do. I would scream it when the anxiety would reach a climax. I chose to believe it when I did not feel it. And I chose to believe it again and again and again until my heart believed it was true.

So darling, if you think you are not enough because of your illness, your ability or inability, your mate or lack of mate, your sin or struggles, hear this today, from God: "You are Enough. As you are. Right Now. Always." You have not blown anything. There is so much more to come.

Navigating Relationships

With this innate desire to self-preserve, I was hoping I would go through this darkness, and then emerge as a butterfly. So I often isolated myself, partly due to my own pride, and partly due to friends not understanding the severity or not bothering to ask. Because of this, I leaned heavily on my relationship with my husband. Since we were supposed to be one, and it was "in sickness and in health," I expected him to be my husband, cheerleader, best friend, researcher, dad to our kid, and take on all the roles I had filled: cleaner, cooker, scheduler, mindful one, booboo kisser, child wrangler, and dog walker. I am not sure why I was surprised when he failed to meet my expectations and did not mindfully pick up on things that needed to be done. Shocker.

Now, I cannot blame all this on Hashimoto's. My real issue in relationships started far before. I felt as if I did not have many friends growing up. I gravitated towards relationships with males instead because I knew that game better. If I keep you somewhat interested in me, but aloof and non-committal, you will hang around to see if you have a chance. Deep insecurity made sure I held other females at a distance, did not trust well, felt sure they were always talking behind my back, and put too much pressure on the relationships I did have.

So I competed with my female comrades. I think most of us did as we grew up. I am so over-the-top excited that this sense of competition between females is now a talking point. I am thrilled my little girl will grow up in a society that says, "Make girls your ally, not your enemy." It's powerful and so overdue. There is room at the table for all of us. But sometimes it just takes another girl to move her chair over and push yours next to hers.

Most of my life was spent with superficial male relationships, fragmented female relationships, and the inability to ask for help or guidance due to my perfectionism. All of this resulted in emotional isolation. Pain has a very funny way of breaking things, though, causing you to re-evaluate and regroup. The first pain was not Hashimoto's, but rather, infertility. I would go to my infertility clinic at 7:00 am, get real intimate with a random stranger as they spent what seemed like hours with a wand up my hoo-ha, then drive across town to my job as an attorney advocate for abused children. Oh, the sweet irony of not being able to have a child and being in the courtroom with a mother who clearly could not help but have kids. It was brutal. I realized right then and there if I was going to survive this season I was going to need friends. Real friends, ride or die types. I would need to throw off my four-inch heels and put on vulnerability instead.

But sometimes you forget lessons learned. Because your body follows the course of least pain and resistance. So you go back to the well-worn path. That is where I found myself in year three of my diagnosis. Feeling very alone and living with a husband who had had enough.

Ladies, it is so important to find a group of women that can support you when you go through tough times. I am in no way advocating for hiding your emotions from your husband or not communicating. I am just saying, in the words of my counselor, "You're not going to get great bread at Home Depot." Do you get that? If your husband is not able to emotionally provide what you may need, you will need to find it elsewhere. The mind will demand an outlet for release. So you must discover productive and healthy ways for that to happen. Go to a women's bible study. Find solid married women who love their husbands and hang out with them. Get a therapist. Join a support group. Do video messaging with your girlfriends. Because if you do not find healthy ways to express your emotions, you are in danger of a failed marriage, resentment, or even infidelity.

We need places to let down our guards, where were can say, "This is me, this is all I got, is it enough?" And the answer needs to be "Yes." My husband was my Home Depot for a while. His inability to deal with his own thoughts about my diagnosis and failed expectations left him desperate for release and bitter. Plus, he was not the open-up type, but rather "let's just be happy, ok?" I have a lot, and I mean a lot of feelings, so this did not jive well. Resentment built up because I did not guard my thoughts about my husband. I let the wild thoughts run rampant of "I am going through all of this, my whole life has changed, and YOU are pissed???!!! You piece of _____.". You get the picture. I love my husband, but I cannot change him. Lord, the only person who has ever changed a man, is Jesus Christ himself. Can I get an Amen, married women?

So let's go back to guarding your thoughts about your husband. Ladies, we are at war with a very real devil, with a very real agenda against families and in particular, marriage. The point of marriage is not for companionship and sex, although those are both excellent things, it was created by God to show the world an example of His love in physical form. It's not about us. So what example are you setting for your kid, for your neighbor, for your family? Do you spend more time complaining about your mate then praying for him? What are your thoughts toward him? You may have every reason in the world to be bitter with your husband. Maybe he was unfaithful. Perhaps he has not been supportive during this challenging season of your life. Or he has not stepped up as a man of God. All of these things will leave you angry and resentful. But listen, justified anger and justified resentment are still anger and resentment. It leaves *you* at a loss, not your husband. It poisons your mind and heart, and harbored, toxic emotions only lead to more sickness in the body. So then you are your own worst enemy. This is not about letting your husband off the hook for bad behavior. On the contrary, it is merely handing him over to a higher court for judgment. God will deal with your husband; you have enough to handle.

I let the negative thoughts toward my husband become my truth about him. The thought "He seems happier when he is at work" became the lie "I am not enough and never will be." The thought "He never helps out around the house without being asked twenty times" became the lie "I can't depend on him. I am on my own." And so on. These negative thoughts began to pile up. He is a firefighter, so I would miss him for the twenty-four hours he was gone, and then he would walk in the door in the morning, and I would be immediately on guard. My reactions to his missteps would be disproportional to the offense. I knew this, yet I felt like I could not stop the behavior and words that flew out of my mouth. Unforgiveness had its nasty stank breath all over this. So when you work from home and the person you see the most is your mate who is off work for forty-eight hours from his shift, it leads to a lot of uncomfortable moments as we passed each other in the hallway.

That is when I asked myself this straightforward question: "Is this worth it?" I am 100 percent justified in my responses to him. He may even deserve it. But it is worth it? Do I like myself more when I act this way? Do I feel closer to God when I compare myself to my husband and come out on top? Does this cold shoulder approach really work for our kid?" And the answer was a resounding "NO."

Since I had a snowball's chance in hell of changing him, I had to change myself. Better yet, I needed to let God change my heart and thoughts toward him. God wants your marriage to succeed. He wants to heal your hearts and bring you closer together. Marriage is his greatest showcase of His power when two very imperfect, broken people can live together in a place of peace and harmony and show love to each other and the world. It's truly beautiful. He also knows it's stupidly hard. So He is waiting with bated breath to help us when we ask for it. So ask for help. Pray hard for your own healing, pray desperately for the healing of your mate's heart and ask God to bring you closer together than you ever have. Ask for a great sex life. No ha-ha here. Do it (pun intended). Nothing good will He withhold from you. That is His promise (Psalms 84:11 NIV). Stop believing the feelings of isolation. Stop limiting God and the healing He can do in your marriage. Start pursuing the heart of your mate and guard your thoughts. This process will feel so much better as a united front.

If you aren't married, you are in no way at a deficit. Marriage is not easy, and it requires continual self-sacrifice and work. So do not feel as if somehow you will not have what you need to get through this time because you don't have a steady partner. Girl, the best conversations and life-giving moments I have ever experienced often have not been with my husband. I love him, and God bless him he tries, but in-depth, soul extending, long, theological bed talk isn't his thing. The tribe of women I have built to support me have been stable anchors through this time. They have spoken life when I was drowning. They have sat with me and cried with me, and sent meaningful and funny memes to brighten my day. They have genuinely prayed for me and rejoiced with me. They have been the most significant lifeline. Do not discredit friendship, and do not sell it short. "Friends come and go, but a true friend sticks by you like family" (Proverbs 18:24 The Message).

I did not have many close female friendships, and I knew I wanted companionship, so I started praying for God to open doors. I decided to get way outside my introvert comfort zone, and group texted three random girls whom I had superficial relationships with but thought they could empathize with my current situation. I initially thought it had been a flop because there was so little momentum at first, but now, I am not sure what I would do without them. We started video messaging each other and little by little our guards came down and life and freedom was spoken out and received. Find your tribe, ladies. The wisest man I know always says, "Life is about relationships." We cannot do this alone. We are not alone. Pray and build your team.

Do I Really Want God?

I think it's worth a chapter to dive into these two thoughts: Do you want God or just His stuff?

I feel like it is easier to understand the God relationship from the position of a marriage or a dedicated human relationship. Because that is what He wants after all: a genuine relationship. The keys to a healthy marriage are a balance of communication, sex, and finances. The same is true for God: prayer, intimacy with the Holy Spirit, and spiritual gains.

If you are engaged in seeking all these things with and for God, you are on a concrete road to a solid relationship with him. The problems come in, whether in a marriage or relationship with God, where these become unbalanced.

You won't have a great marriage if you don't share responsibilities with your spouse, and you will not thrive in your relationship with God if you just keep asking Him to do things for you. There has to be balance. God is not a puppet master nor a genie; neither is your spouse. If either were acting in this manner, then you would be in an abusive or codependent relationship, and you need to get out.

How do you know if you want God or just His stuff? Just ask yourselves these questions: How do I deal with flare-ups? How do I deal with life's disappointments or confusion? Do I tend to fall apart? Do I blame God? Do I feel like I am on an emotional rollercoaster? Do I feel easily swayed, and hate it?

I was totally there, sister. Getting dizzy after every loop-di-loop, wanting to desperately get off the ride. Sick of the free-fall after every disappointment. Never confident I could handle the next obstacle. Just holding on. That is not the freedom for which He has set us free. That's not freedom at all. We get like this because, though we may love God very much, what we are ultimately most enthused with is His stuff. His magic wand. The things He can change or fix or bless us with. We go up and down and all around on the roller coaster because we most likely have not understood His perfect love and His character. We have not settled in our hearts the truths of His word and the promises. We have not fully believed what God said about Himself. So we are blindsided and left doubting when a long-awaited thing does not seem to come, or even this illness. Because we forgot who God is, and now all we want is His stuff. If this sounds like you at all, that's okay. This is where growth happens.

Our marriage counselor once told my husband and me the most significant and most annoying bit of advice. He said, "No matter what has happened, you need to start with the thought that your spouse loves you and that you need to impute good to all of his actions." Meaning, you need to assume your spouse is not a narcissist and was, in fact, trying to do something nice and is not actively trying to piss you off or hurt you. Bless our therapist, but the struggle-bus train has entered the station. But he is 100 percent right. That is precisely what I need to do with my spouse. I know I did not marry Charles Manson, and I know he loves me, so I need to assume all, and I mean ALL of his actions are somehow in his mind for my good. It would stop so many pointless arguments over miscommunications and hurt feelings. It would make me see my husband in a positive light. It would make me so less dang sensitive. I would be lighter, and our marriage would benefit. It would be healing for me, for us.

So how do you start to want God? You believe He loves you. That He wants good things for you. That all of His actions are for your good; and that if something terrible happens because of other humans or a broken world, then He will turn it all around for your good, and I mean ALL. Then you could rest in your trust of Him that it will all turn out okay. You would not have to question Him so much. You would rest easier, literally. You would be at great peace. You would be lighter, and your relationship with God would blossom. It would be healing for you. You would finally get off that roller coaster and land on the solid ground of faith and trust and say: "I am not in control, but You are, and I believe Your promises, so I will stand firm in You because You will come through." And it would be true. No matter how horrendous the plotline seems to be. He will finish that story, and it will end in redemption. Every. Single. Time.

I think the phrase "seeking and finding God" simply means this: bringing true head knowledge of God to your heart. There is not a single thing written in this book that is novel or unique. This has all been said multiple times before by far more eloquent people. But all it takes is that one time. The one time where it finally clicks, and you realize, "I trust this now. This has become a part of my belief system. I am all in on this." When your heart rests in your beliefs of God, you, sister, have found Him.

God wants you to want Him, oftentimes so you can more clearly see His stuff, the blessings we are daily missing because we are struggling to believe there is a good plan in all of this.

May you find Him. He wants you. Get off the roller coaster and stand firm in His arms. He has you.

New Memories

"How are you feeling? What happened? Do you think this is all just in your head? Explain in detail your medical history," remarks the random stranger with no medical credentials who I just met at a friend's birthday party.

Do you get these impertinent questions too? It's invasive, exhausting, and frustrating to rehash your medical history. I often find it easier to answer, "I'm doing okay." It's not a lie. I just don't want to go there. The hot tears are always at the door, and I don't want to get that vulnerable while I'm just trying to eat confetti cake. I don't want to think about the last flare-up, I just want to survive it. I don't want to think about the day I was diagnosed. I don't want to replay the fear I felt when I was hospitalized for the first time, and I was sent home with the knowledge I had something suspicious on my thyroid and cancer was whispered. I don't want to think about the days in dark rooms with body tremors and whispered prayers to survive. It's just too much to relive those memories.

But refusing to process something consciously does not make the memories go away. If anything, it makes them a magnified toxic ball of emotions my subconscious is left to wade through. So the pain and fear become even more ingrained, and the body's avoidance response to these stimuli becomes unbearable. Now not talking about our chronic illness is a matter of survival. Often, we feel as if we are brave or strong by not talking about it. We don't want to be a bother or a life suck. We want to pretend it's not happening. This is not our life. We don't want to bother our spouses because we carry so much guilt for our diagnosis, and so we try to bottle things up until we explode with emotion. We don't want our children to see us struggle, so we put on brave faces and push ourselves even when we know we should self-care and rest. Please tell me this is not just me?

I was in my car, listening to my Spotify Station "Bethel Music" when the spontaneous, live version of the song *Pieces* by Bethel Music came on. I do my best worshipping while alone in my car. I really get into it. I am sure many traffic cameras have caught what looks to be a maniac with one hand up in the air, the other on the wheel hysterically crying. Yep, that's me driving down the highway, singing to my God, pouring my heart and pain out in song. It's my go-to release. In *Pieces*, the lead singer, Steffany Gretzinger, starts softly sing-speaking, "You're giving us new memories. All the places shame wrote our story. You're giving us Your memory. It's not just perspective. It's innocence restored. You're rewriting our story. Our story with your love."[6] As my car kept going, my mind stopped dead in its tracks. Was that possible? Could God really give me a new memory to replace a haunting memory? Not just changing the way I view things because I am more Zen now, but legitimately the way God viewed the situation that I cannot shake from my subconscious? It broke me, y'all. I wanted that more than anything right then. I needed new memories. And the key to unlocking this precious gift: prayer. God does not want you to be a victim of your memories. He does not intend for us to be tormented by our memories. God does not want His children to be broken by the thought of their own bad decisions or decisions made against their will. So whether by your own doing, the carelessness of others with your heart, or the disgusting acts of evil, you are creating your private prison if you keep replaying the memories without the mercy of God and His peace washing over them.

So I prayed this exact prayer:

"Lord, forgive me for my distrust and doubt of You. My reliance on my own strength and self. For believing the returning lie that I am alone and have to do this alone. I'm sorry for my doubt of Your love and for doubting Your ability to heal and see me through. I declare that the past is in the past. It does not have permission to touch me anymore. It is done, I am free. There's a statute of limitations here. I live by grace and am forgiven of this already. I am so loved and cared for and have everything inside me already that I need. I am not disqualified because of this. I don't live in shame anymore. I claim Your power in my spirit. I claim love, joy, peace, resilience, gentleness, goodness, faith, meekness, and self-control. I ask for the freedom to deflect lies and embrace Your truth instead. I believe You for this healing of my memories and mind. Thank you for grace, and my innocence restored. Amen."

I know God can and will do this because He has for me. The first time God gave me a new memory was in my deepest shame. I was just told I was going to be a mother for the first time and I would need to get on a plane within twenty-four hours to meet my daughter. I was awash in emotion, excitement, fear, excitement, terror, joy, did I mention excitement? It all happened so quickly, I could barely catch my breath. We showed up at the house of a charming Australian nanny the next night, and as she went into the next room to get our daughter, I was holding back fear tears. "Did I know what to do?" I suddenly felt very much like a kid myself, could I care for a newborn? The nanny placed my baby in my arms, and I held her with wide eyes of disbelief. My husband snapped a picture of me while I held her and stared.

During her "sip and see" weeks later, my parents had printed out all the pictures we had taken already and framed them as a surprise. It was a beautiful gift. But every time I would look at those pictures in my house and on my walls, I would feel such tremendous guilt. I had wanted to be a mother for such a long time. I had just received the greatest blessing my hands had ever held up to that point, and I felt fear?! I hated that my first memory of my precious blessing was tainted this way. In tears, I begged God one day, "Show me what You saw that day." And He did. I was taken back to that moment in time, but this time I was the observer. I was above the scene looking in, and I saw myself holding my little girl. But I felt the love of God washing over everything this time. The feeling that comes in the air when the divine works such a beautiful redemption that it is palpable, and I smiled. I saw what God saw. Love. Now every single time I bring up that memory, I see what God saw, I feel what He felt. I received His memory.

God will do this for you too. I know it. So receive this blessing today: "May the God who loves every single thing about you, even the worst of you, give you the view from His own eyes of everything that has ever wrecked you, and may you walk out of your prison with new memories of love and forgiveness."

Rethinking the Whale

The story of Jonah almost seems too other-worldly to be true, like a scene out of Harry Potter. You have this guy, who appears to be a melancholy lad by the tone you get from his words and actions. The God of the universe speaks directly to him and says: "Go tell the people of Nineveh an important message." But Jonah gets pissed, and like a petulant child pouts and says, "I don't want to go there. I don't want to do that. This was not my choice." So Jonah mic-drops and heads in the opposite direction in the ultimate four-year-old move of na-na-na-boo-boo, you can't catch me. But not shockingly, God does, and decides to capture Jonah's attention by sending a hurricane-like storm to scare the crap out of the sailors and the captain of the boat Jonah chose to run away on. To understand the enormity of this storm, you have to recognize that these are seafaring men, their lives and years were spent on the sea, and they were crapping themselves in fear. And in the midst of all of this chaos, what does Jonah do? He decides to take a nap. Remember, this is no luxury ocean liner. This is a wooden ship with maybe hammocks to sleep in. There has to be a crazy high level of emotional checking-out to be able to sleep through that.

The captain goes below deck, and wakes Jonah up by screaming, "Cry out to your god, man." But Jonah stays quiet, and God does not relent. At this point, Jonah had the opportunity to pray to God. To relent and surrender. To ask for forgiveness and listen to God.

I feel quite confident God would have stopped the storm, just like that. The storm was not sent as a punishment; the storm was sent as a deterrent. But Jonah refuses out of stubbornness and pride. The still freaking-out sailors decide to start casting lots, a fancier game of pick the straw, where they will blame the storm on whoever draws the shorter stick. Jonah obviously loses and then openly admits, "Sorry guys, this storm is because I did not listen to God."

Did you catch that? Jonah knew the whole time the storm was about him. Not just some random act of bad luck on the seas. He knew. Again, Jonah could have owned up. Again, Jonah could have asked for forgiveness and listened to God. But our stubborn and seemingly depressed boy says, "Let me die, throw me overboard." Either this is the most stubborn man in the Bible, or he really had a messed up view of the love and grace of God. I am willing to go out on a plank (see what I did there?) and say the latter. So overboard he goes. Jonah is actively drowning when a massive whale comes up and swallows Jonah whole. The end. I mean, at this point, why not, God? Why is Jonah worth all of this trouble? Pick someone else to take your message. Like there is no other person in the world who could say the words You wanted Jonah to say??? But in His mercy, follow me here, God sent a whale. The whale was Jonah's salvation. He would have drowned in the middle of that ocean because of his decision to hold onto his stubborn pride. But God sent His salvation in the form of a whale to not harm him, but protect him until he reached dry land.

So what is your whale? For a long time, my whale was my diagnosis. It was the giant thing that swallowed me whole, and it trapped me. I could not see how good could come from anything this terrible. I could not fathom mercy and salvation through this. It was just a horrible, awful whale.

Before my diagnosis, I was in the rat race, busting my behind, living a productive but joyless life, working hard for good things, but not the things that were good for me. I never filled my own cup. I thought self-care was a cop-out. I thought rest was for weak people. I did not value quiet time. I couldn't nap, no matter how tired I was. There was never an off switch. I lived in stress mode, and I called it normal. Honestly, I was on a path to dying of a heart attack by the age of sixty. But God sent a whale. This diagnosis forced me to slow down, to re-evaluate what I put my energy into. It caused me to sit. It required me to face my thoughts. To establish rest. To reinvent my normal. Honestly, I resented the crap out of this for years. Because in my twisted mind, rest took away time for me to achieve, and I am an achiever. I kicked, railed, and fought against this whale with every bit of bitterness I could muster.

But God did not relent. He, in His mercy, said, "This growth and breakoning is worth it." So He allowed me to sit there for three years while I ran and hid. Until little by little, I learned to surrender. I started small by practicing at-home yoga (Yoga with Adriene will change your life. Google her). I started meditating. I started setting a twenty-minute timer and forced myself to lay down and focus on my breathing, not my thoughts. I began to plan my days sparingly. I began to see the value in "me time" and self-care. I permitted myself to take time-outs. I slowed my pace and breath when life began to feel like it was spinning. I started coloring and painting rocks. I stopped watching most TV and limited my phone time. And then one day, rest did not feel so bad. The chaotic pace felt foreign.

We can continue to look at our whale with anger and resentment. We can let it continue to swallow us whole. Or, we can choose to see it for the salvation that it is. Romans 8:28 (NIV) says, "We know that all things work together for good to them that love God, to them who are the called according to His purpose." Regardless if it feels good all the time, it is good. By good, I do not mean happy. God is not working all things together for our feel-good happiness. There are plenty of things I require my child to do and direct her not to do for her good. This leads to much moaning and gnashing of teeth from her because she cannot have candy for breakfast. But my child's happiness is not my highest goal for her. God works in the same way. He takes the brokenness caused by our misgivings or the brutality of others and makes something good come out of it. It's a promise filled with hope. God will pursue you. You don't need to worry about whether you can handle your struggles. You are never being called to be perfect, so you don't start a flare-up from stress or feel so overwhelmed with emotions. God is just saying, give it to me. I'll handle it so you don't have to. You don't have to worry about getting it all right all the time. The right medicine, supplements, food, exercise, attitude. God is invested. If you stick with Him, "Whether you turn to the right or to the left, your ears will hear a voice behind you, saying, 'This is the way; walk in it'" (Isaiah 30:21 NIV). This whale can be your salvation, if you let it. God will stop at nothing to save you, even from yourself. Psalm 139:7-11 (NIV) reaffirms this when it says, "Where can I go from your Spirit? Where can I flee from your presence? If I go up to the heavens, you are there; if I make my bed in the depths, you are there. If I rise on the wings of the dawn, if I settle on the far side of the sea, even there your hand will guide me, your right hand will hold me fast. If I say, 'Surely the darkness will hide me, and the light become night around me,' even the darkness will not be dark to you; the night will shine like the day, for darkness is as light to you." He will never stop saving you and leading back on the right path.

So no matter what your whale is, you can trust God that it will bring you to dry ground in His time. You are worth this trouble. You are worth the pursuit. He has an extraordinary plan only you can complete. You are His Jonah.

Section Two
Spring

Enapay

We decided on our daughter's middle name while on a plane ride to Arizona. We had been told less than twenty-four hours prior that we had been chosen by the birth mother to be her parents and we needed to come as soon as possible to meet our baby girl. I sent a text message to my boss that I was going on maternity leave (I am not kidding). And off we went. I was sleeping on my husband's arm while in flight, woke up, and blurted out, "Enapay, her middle name is going to be Enapay." Our baby girl is Native American, and Enapay is the Sioux word for Brave. If any little girl was going to need one skill to make it well in this world, it was going to be bravery.

I had lost hope that we would ever have a child, so when we did adopt our little darling, things got real. How do I raise a girl in a world like this? It's so brutal. And social media can be a real kick in the ovaries to a girls' self-esteem. Now there's not just mean girls, but cyberbullies??? Jesus take the wheel. I felt ill-equipped. Not that it is easier on the boys; God knows they have their own struggles. But growing up with an XX chromosome, I knew how tricky it could be.

When I first got sick, I was so angry with God for allowing this to happen to my baby girl. I mean, I went through infertility, then in-vitro treatment, failed in-vitro, then signed with one adoption agency, then another, and then finally a baby. And I was hand-picked by God to be her mother. And then I got sick? I was struggling for a hot minute to even care for myself, let alone an eighteen-month-old human. Why? It seemed heartless and senseless. But when the rage cries cleared away, do you know what I was left with on the crappiest of days? A little girl with big brown eyes who wanted to be cuddled, who only would allow *me* to rock her to sleep; who gave the sweetest hugs and kisses. I was left with strength because guess what? I could do this for her. I had no choice but to soldier on, because of her—what a gift.

In the breakoning years that followed my diagnosis, I read the life-changing book *Brave, Not Perfect* by Reshma Saujani to become a more enlightened mother. I mean, I gave my daughter the middle name of Enapay for God's sake. I needed to figure out how to foster that in her. If, at a job interview, they asked me to list my three greatest attributes, bravery was never, ever going to come out of my mouth. I did not take chances because I could fail, and failure meant a lack of perfection, and that meant the world was ending (apparently, I could list drama as an attribute). So, I am reading this book when it starts to feel like the author has been following me. This woman knew my whole life. I felt so exposed. Her message was profound. Women in their thirties are coming to crises in their lives, and a rise in anxiety and depression has set in with this population. Why? Because women were taught how to be perfect. Life has played out as it does, and we realize it can suck and be hard, and there sometimes is nothing we can do about it. Our coping mechanism was perfection, and that has failed us, so we don't know what to do with the broken pieces, and unfortunately, we never developed resilience. Because resilience required failure, and that was not allowed. But, we can develop needed resilience now by being brave.[7]

Tribe, it was like my head exploded. My eyes were opened and I knew I needed to be rebuilt. I started my bravery practice by doing something new each day that kinda scared me or put me out of my comfort zone. I am not talking about bungee jumping, y'all.

I'm talking about small things like pushing my body to go a little further on my morning walk with my dog and taking my daughter to the Science Center by myself. I did not realize how weak I had made myself out to be. The limitations I had put on myself. The way I had worn the scarlet letter of "sick girl" on my chest. The martyrdom pedestal I was resting on. Bravery became a new anthem. A calling. Do it, even if it scares you, because it scares you.

Now hear me well: I am not advocating for recklessness or pushing yourself beyond a point where you hurt yourself or become sicker. That's not bravery, that's stupidity. Bravery will be different for each of us. My husband is a firefighter, so he gets mad when he misses a house fire or any chance to run inside a burning building with scorching temperatures because he is *loco*. Although most people would look at him and say that's brave, that is not bravery for my husband. It does not scare him to go into the fire, but you know what does cause his knees to shake? Having a vulnerable conversation with an acquaintance. You see what I am getting at? Extroverts are not the only brave people in the world. If you are battling with social anxiety, going to the party or concert is your bravery. If you quit a stable job to start your own business, that is your bravery. Deciding to go to counseling and deal with your fears and issues is probably the highest form of bravery there is.

I realized I could not teach my daughter a skill I did not possess myself. If I wanted her to be my little Enapay, I needed to be that as well. So I went to counseling. I went to the concerts. I started my own interior decorating business, Enapay Designs. I was scared crapless. But I did it anyway. Because I am learning my bravery. I am realizing it is okay to fail, and I should fail often, so I can grow. I am doing this for her and mostly for me. Because I am brave no matter what that looks like. So are you. Go forth and be Enapay.

What Are You Walking Out of Egypt With?

Is it of little wonder most people who have been diagnosed with an auto-immune disorder or chronic illness also struggle with anxiety or depression. Yes, the diagnosis itself with its bent toward hormonal imbalance is the first strike. But there is also the coming to terms with the knowledge that henceforth, life may need to look a little different. There may be some limitations now. There may be more days of recovery or rest, which may feel like your life now has to be less fun or full of adventure. As a parent, you may feel like you can't keep up with your kids as you had hoped, or you may not be able to have more children as you had desired. This can be through infertility or physical ability. As a wife, you may feel like this has put a significant damper on your sex life and desire to be touched because you are in pain more often than you would like. Or maybe your mate doesn't understand, and the ignorance and side-eye are so hurtful to you. All and any one of these things could cause the average duck to lose hope. And yes, this diagnosis may last a lifetime, but this is just a season. I say this with all confidence.

God may not give you the miraculous healing you so desperately pray for, but He will provide you with freedom, a sound mind, peace, love, joy, perseverance, goodness, faith, and self-control (Galatians 5:22 NIV). This means we can overcome our fears, anxiety, and depression. We have a choice, and mercy, wouldn't we like more of those, am I right? I did not choose to have this diagnosis, and for a very, very long time I allowed it to fill me with so much fear and anxiety I could barely stand some days. I was a prisoner to the disease. I did not have it; it had me.

I had no clue how to trust God. I literally did not know what that meant. I needed a twelve-step plan. A manual to show me how to do it. I knew I was in over my head and way past my strength's ability to keep up the fight. God was there. He actually had never left. I was just too dang busy trying to fix myself to see He was waiting patiently for me to exhaust myself and surrender. Understand this, though: God did not need me to exhaust myself and surrender before stepping in. I needed this. I needed to feel like I was the author of my destiny and in control of EVERYTHING. Since God is pro-choice, He allowed me to make that decision. It wasn't the right one, but He allows it all the same. We are not puppets.

I hit my rock bottom after I was diagnosed with the pituitary brain tumor. It was one too many fear zones colliding at once. This is where I finally understood, "The Lord will fight for you; you need only to be still" (Exodus 14:14 NIV). God goes before me to fight off the enemy of my soul and mind. So to fortify this message, I conjured up an image in my mind of a battle scene, *Braveheart* style. I am standing with a banner raised over my head. On the banner is written every victory God has ever had on my behalf. I am in my full armor, and my face is painted fierce. And God and His Angel Armies are running full force at the approaching army, as I lift up my voice and praise Him through words and songs. Cheering Him on, screaming His victory, declaring the defeat of the enemy and God's win. Go ahead, put this book down and take a moment to imagine your battle scene. I'm not kidding. What does it look like for you to have God fight your battles?

When Pharaoh told the Israelites they were free from centuries of slavery, God pressed upon the Egyptians to be generous in their gift-giving, upon request. So when packing up for their unknown journey, the now recently freed slaves went to their prior captors and said "give me all the cookies, all the jewels, glitter me up, pretty please with a cherry on top." God opened the hearts and arms of the Egyptians to be generous because He was not about to have His children leave their time in slavery without spoils, if they asked.

But the Israelites were quickly catapulted back into the fear zone as they stood at the banks of the Red Sea, and Pharaoh and his armies were charging forward to kill and enslave again. I am sure they were terrified. But Moses gets up before them and tells them not to be afraid because the God of the Angel Armies will defeat their approaching enemy; they just need to stand still and watch the salvation unfold. God opened the sea like a book, and Moses says, "Now walk through."

The Israelites had a choice, though. They could have turned on Moses and said they were going to take their chances and surrender to Pharaoh and go back to Egypt. Egypt is what they knew, the already worn path in their minds and bodies. They knew what to expect in Egypt, and even if it was terrible, it was still better than the unknown. They could have refused to walk through the Red Sea and stayed back on the shores. I don't know about you, but it seems freakin' terrifying to walk between two massive curtains of water and into a dessert. But understand this: Your enemy does not want you to leave your slavery. He wants you to remain in fear, anxiety, and depression. Because when we are operating out of these zones, we are the most self-focused.

Sometimes walking out of Egypt means getting into regular counseling, medicine or supplements, talking to trusted, wise friends, or a mix of these. These, too, are miracles. These are not marks of a lack of faith or trust. God uses these modalities most of the time to help you walk to freedom. But freedom always includes learning to trust God, and you learn how to trust God by stating the truth, out loud, to yourself, and then determining to actually believe it. Then watch and wait for God's next move. And I promise you,

God will move. He will change your heart and thoughts in beautiful ways, usually not all at once, but over time. You will learn to partner with Him. Doing it on your own will start to feel foreign. Your desire for His presence will grow, and you will seek it out. You will begin guarding your thoughts, like a momma bear with her cubs. Lies will come, and you will learn to beat them down with all force and say, "God, I give this to you." This takes time, grace, and truth, truth, truth.

So let's start with some great truths:
- God loves you as you are.
- You can control your thoughts with the help of God.
- You are not a victim of your condition.
- You have an enemy, remember that.
- You are enough. As you are. Right now. Always.
- You are not being punished.
- Your life is not over.
- This is a new beginning.
- It won't always be like this.
- You will grow in strength and resolve the more you combat the toxic thoughts.

So you have a choice: Will this disease continue to take more from you than it already has? Will you choose to be a victim or a banner-waving warrior? You can walk out of Egypt with freedom, joy, peace, self-control, resilience, stronger faith and trust, and one hell of a testimony, or you can stay behind. What's it going to be? Slave or free? I hope you choose to leave the slavery of your mind behind and take all of the spoils God is waiting to give you. You just need to ask.

Self-Care

I am an advocate at heart. You show me a pet rescue commercial with Sarah McLaughlin playing in the background, I will raise you a house full of dogs the next day. I am allergic to cats, but do you think I was going to let a little thing like breathing get in the way of me raising five feral kittens when their mother abandoned them? Get out of here with that nonsense. I will help until I need help. And folks, that isn't a good thing.

I knew I should have stepped away from my work as a child advocate two years before I actually did. I knew it in my heart, but I was doing "so much good" and "they needed me." Hear this: Just because you are doing something good does not make it right for you. I could feel tiredness and stress in my body. The weekend was not enough to remediate all the strain I had put on it throughout the week. My immune system could not keep up with this tremendous load, and so began to fail. But I soldiered through. After the adoption of our child, I just added on "new mom" to the plate but did not take anything off it. I could handle it. I cleaned my house neurotically. I worked from home with a baby lying next to me. I slept poorly and could not nap because I never learned the skill of chill.

I was a dutiful mom, and as such, I never took time away from our new bundle of joy. I thought this is how it was supposed to be. Exhausted mother giving her all for her kid. I wore dark circles around my eyes like a badge of honor and resigned myself to love my daughter, but maybe not really liking this stage in my life and enduring. I was a blast to be around, I am sure.

Ladies, the thing is this: Self-care is an act of worship. God tells us our bodies are temples (1 Corinthians 6:19 NIV). The home of the divine. And God prioritized rest by giving us a Sabbath day. Giving us the permission we need to say, "That laundry can wait. I need to rest." But often God's approval does not seem to matter to us. We hold the validity of others as a higher mark to achieve. Or better yet, we refuse to give ourselves our own permission to stop the roller coaster of achievement. We hold ourselves to the Instagram/Pinterest standard. Can you relate or have you fallen prey to one or more of the following?

- Carefully curating your pictures with the right filters and angles.
- Making your child's last birthday more expensive and/or more highly decorated than your wedding.
- Feeding your family only organic, Paleo meals. Or better yet, daily themed lunch boxes with crust-free, shaped sandwiches.
- Engaging in Joanna Gaines-level decorating, but with only two cents to rub together because paying full price is so gauche.

Listen, I am not knocking any of these things as bad or ungodly. I do all of them. I love taking pictures of my family because my little girl is so stinking cute, and I needed you to see how she "did her own hair today." Also, I use filters simply because I want to look flattering in them because God has not cured me of my vanity yet. Prayers appreciated. I love my kid, and I love planning. So yeah, her birthday parties are a bit over the top. I also believe, like Ann Wigmore, that "The food [we] eat can be either the safest and most powerful form of medicine or the slowest form of poison." I also started an interior design company for crying out loud. Are you going to take advice on window treatments from a woman who uses bed sheets hung up with push pins? Nonsense.

But I do these things, not because I am compelled by some outside force and need to impress. I do these things because I love them. Because they bring me joy and life. You know what's not on my joy list?

- Doing elaborate Marie Antoinette hairstyles for my kid. I bribe her with organic gummy bears (because somehow they are better for you) and comb her hair. If I manage to get a simple braid or two in there, I am parent-winning.
- Creating sensory boxes and experiments for my kid to broaden her mind. It's admirable. I have all the intentions in the world of doing it, but then I don't. Honestly, I am totally okay with this. She is going to be hilarious and sarcastic anyway, so no need for book smarts.
- Makeup tutorials, contouring, and coloring in my eyebrows. This is just witchcraft.
- Multi-step date nights with my husband. I love him. He is my best friend, but by evening this momma is tired and is at best putting on heels, will make out in the car and in bed by 10:00 p.m.

We all have things that we are rock stars at or just fill us up whether or not we excel at them. Do those things. Invest in those things. Leave the rest for your judgmental mother-in-law. You are doing your best, not someone else's best.

You may be wondering what your thing is. Awesome, you aren't alone. I had spent so much of my life trying to figure out what others wanted from me or wanted me to be, I forgot to figure out what I liked. So I basically went through a rebellion in my thirties. Got henna tattoos, colored and cut my hair however I wanted, tried out bold shades of lipstick, found the clothing style I love on my body, became a yogi, and questioned everything.

This is the start of self-care. Finding out what you love. What gets your blood flowing and passions firing on all cylinders. What do you find yourself smiling while doing? Next, do that thing as often as possible.

But what about those things that are selfish? Like going out with girlfriends even if the kids are still up and your husband had a bad day at work? Or getting or giving yourself a manicure or pedicure. What about a massage by the hands of a masseuse and not your hubby looking for some action; and dare I even say it, frequently? Taking a long bubble bath with the door locked and music on. Going shopping by yourself for yourself. I'm not talking about a TP run to Target. I am talking about your favorite clothing shop to buy yourself and only yourself something you feel beautiful in. Letting Netflix watch your child a little longer than you were hoping because you need to re-center yourself. Are you picking up the strong sarcasm? THESE ARE NOT SELFISH.

I can hear it now: "You don't understand, money is tight because I had to lower my hours at work, take a pay cut, or stop working altogether because of this disease and so I can't be any more of a burden financially to my family." I get it. I really do. I did not work for almost two years after I was diagnosed. I felt all of those guilts and toxic burden thoughts. But it's lies we are telling ourselves. Sit down with your husband and go over the discretionary budget and carve out some money for your own needed self-care. Allow your mate to do the same. Be creative. If you aren't, go to Pinterest for a step-by-step process on how to paint flowers on your toenails. When it fails miserably, laugh and take a picture and send it to your girlfriends. It was worth it just to try. Remembering who you are is so important when you are dealing with chronic illness. So fill your time with things that bring out your truest self.

Self-care

Self-care is not selfish. Listen to this again! SELF-CARE IS NOT SELFISH. God loves it. He wants us to take care of ourselves. Our full selves: body, mind, and spirit. Whatever you are battling has, I am sure, already taken a lot from you. Don't be your own worst enemy by colluding with the disease and refusing to care for yourself too. So stop being selfish by NOT taking care of yourself. Here is your permission: Go forth and care.

All the Things[1]

I have a Marco Polo group with three girlfriends. If you aren't familiar with this app, it allows you to leave video messages for your friends to be able to watch at their leisure and respond back. We all live locally, but you know, life, schedules, kids. It's hard to stay connected. But it is so worth it. I love my Marco Polo group. We share deep secrets we have never spoken out loud, funny stories, tears, and tons of advice. It's the best. In one of the Marco messages, my girlfriend said, "Britt, I feel like you do all the things. You are always looking for solutions and trying new things to make yourself better." It was a huge compliment, but honestly, I was left a little speechless. I did not realize it was possible to NOT try all the things. My personality, with its bent towards achievement, has always propelled me forward toward excellence at all costs, and that means never stalemating.

So in the quest of always trying to find solutions and better health or management of it, I may have tried a few things, often guinea pigging myself to see what does and does not work for my condition. There are many different brands of auto-immune diseases, but they often come with similar symptoms of fatigue, pain/discomfort, inflammation, and stress-caused ailments. Because of the commonalities, these suggestions may work even if you do not

---

[1] Disclaimer: I am not a doctor, nor do I play one on television. The following is just a bunch of things that have helped me and may or may not work for you. Always consult with your doctor before you try something new.

have Hashimoto's or Centralized Sensitization Syndrome. So here they are in alphabetical order:

Acupuncture:

A subset of Chinese Medicine where small needles are lightly tapped into key points of the body. Most clinics have soft, low lighting with comfortable chairs and blankets if you get cold. It's recommended to sit with the inserted needles for at least thirty minutes. It can be an incredibly relaxing experience. Testimonials include pain relief, better digestion, better sleep, and emotional balance. Check out https://www.pocacoop.com/clinics/search-by-state for an acupuncture co-op near you. With a co-op experience, you pay a sliding fee typically between $15-$40 dollars per session, and it is always at your discretion. I personally have an intense needle phobia, so it was not as relaxing as I was hoping it would be for me, but many friends have had incredible results, and so it is worth a try.

Ashwagandha and other Adrenal Herbs:

When your body goes through a stressful event, your adrenals are there to help you cope and compensate by providing your body with the necessary energy it needs. But when the stressful event does not abate for an extended period, your adrenals can become tired and may require some support. My wise integrative medicine practitioner saw the writing on the wall and started me on Ashwagandha, an adaptogen herb, when this mess all started. I am so grateful for this. I don't think he or I foresaw how long this battle toward balance would be. But I know that because I took preventative measures, my adrenals have been able to sustain me. Even if you are already in adrenal fatigue, it is still worthwhile to start rebuilding now. As always, ask your doctor before you try anything new.

Cranio-Sacral Therapy:

I was more than a little skeptical of this modality. It's characterized by a feather-light massage on the body to help muscle tension release and the spinal fluid to flow freely. But being the cheapskate I am, I was not about to drop $100 a session on quackery. So when I tell you that Cranio-Sacral Therapy was my only non-negotiable each week, I mean business. It was hands down the best healing modality I tried. My headaches went away. I experienced significantly fewer body pains. I was able to recover from stressful events more quickly, and I released built-up emotions in my body. Two thumbs up from me.

Diet:

There are various diets out there: Keto, Paleo, Whole30, vegan, and so on. Find the one that is right for your body. I recommend you trying these diets to see which one works best for your body. If the thought of this gives you hives, you can try the Autoimmune Protocol, which is basically an elimination diet where you have strict food restrictions and slowly add things back to see how they make you feel. It can really whittle down your sensitivities and show you if you really need to be gluten-free as everyone is screaming about. Thank God for a simple Google search so you now don't have to buy ten books and compare. With the click of a button in an internet search, it can walk you through this protocol and help you get recipes to navigate what is and is not allowed. I found for a while I felt best on a Paleo diet. It helped my digestion and inflammation, and so it was worth it to not go face deep in a bowl of queso. My greatest practice tip: go on Pinterest, type in "Paleo Meals" and build a grocery list from what looks appealing. This will ensure you have the ingredients you need and takes out the guesswork.

Drink Water:

I know you have heard this many times, but that is because it is bona fide advice, and why haven't you listened already?! Your body is comprised of mostly water, and we need to replenish it for the systems in our bodies to work correctly. So listen to your mother and your podcasts, drink your water. The rule is as many ounces as half of your body weight. So if you weigh 150 pounds, then you should need around seventy-five ounces of water. I got a bunch of glass water bottles on Amazon and filled them up, and kept them in the refrigerator for easy access and zero excuses. Start there.

Eye Movement Desensitization and Reprocessing (EMDR) Therapy:

Are you ready to get your butt kicked in therapy? Then EMDR is for you! It's not a great hype game, but it is worth it. The name feels intense and scary, but it truly is not. When someone experiences trauma, the right and left sides of her brain stop communicating. It's just survival. If you don't need it to survive, it's out. So bye-bye long term memory storage. So long digestion. That is why often we have hazy memories of an adverse event in our lives. Don't get tripped up on the word "trauma." We often only equate rape or mass shootings victims as being worthy of the trauma blanket. But that is absolutely not true. We each will experience trauma differently, and each has a different threshold of pain. Hear me on this: Just because your threshold is a bit more sensitive does not mean you are weak. It is genetics and a life narrative colliding together. You are not broken. If it is affecting you, then it's affecting you. Do not try to push it aside because you don't feel like it is "bad enough."

In EMDR therapy, you engage in the counseling process while holding a small buzzer pad in each hand. It is not painful in any way, just a soft vibration. You will begin to discuss past experiences through the leading of a certified therapist, and the pads will buzz back and forth in your hands. This occurs to stimulate the left and right sides of your brain to start communicating, to start the healing process, and get you out of trauma brain. The average session should last around ninety minutes. This therapy jump-started my internal healing for so many things I had put on the shelf and thought were not affecting me. It was a beautiful mess. I highly recommend this if you are ready to be free and healed.

God and Christian Guidance:

All of the modalities listed here are great. If it works for you, keep doing it. I have tried many, and only a few are listed here. But of all the things I poured my time, money, and effort into, none of them have compared to being healed by the God who loves me. I sought out my pastor, who has also been diagnosed with an autoimmune condition, and brought all my questions and anger about God to her. It was so great to hear her perspective. It wasn't that she had all the answers, but that she was confident in who God was, which gave me the courage to keep seeking.

God will speak for Himself. He wants to have a relationship with us. He is not trying to hide Himself. This is not some cosmic game of cat and mouse. The divine within you will guide you to the answers at the right time. Jesus says: "Take my yoke upon you and learn from me, for I am gentle and humble in heart, and you will find rest for your souls" (Matthew 11:28 NIV). He is waiting there for us to want to have a genuine relationship with Him. He will provide the peace you need. But it all begins with surrender and trust. The choices, not the feelings. God will meet you there, and this is where your most significant healing will start. This is the only recommendation that comes with a guarantee of success.

Integrative Medicine and Alternative Medicine:

I have tried holistic medicine, traditional medicine, and also integrative medicine, which is a combination of both traditional medicine with holistic. I had far greater success with integrative medicine. If you are under the care of a holistic practitioner, make sure blood draws are a regular part of your care. All the holistic machines in the world are wonderful, but they do not take the place of confirmation through blood work. I say this from personal experience, as I was under the care of a holistic practitioner for many years, and blood work was never addressed. I spent a lot of money we really did not have on supplements and modalities. When I sought an integrative doctor for a second opinion, the first thing he ordered was a full blood work panel, including thyroid panels. Within a few weeks, I had a diagnosis for what was going on. Based on the subsequent scans, it appeared as if I had had the disease for quite some time. Definitely within the timeframe of being under the care of the holistic practitioner. There may have been preventive or corrective care I could have engaged in to help slow or stop the autoimmune process, but unfortunately it was too late by the time I was diagnosed. I firmly believe in alternative medicine, but there must be a balance.

My integrative doctor is a saint. Yes, it is true that most of them are not covered by insurance. But that is not because the doctors are lazy and don't want to deal with the paperwork, it is because they want to spend quality time with their patients so they can be confident in their treatment goals and have a full picture. It is the care we all need in order to get to the source and not just symptom management. My doctor has fielded calls from me while I have been in the hospital, on the weekend, and when he has been on vacation and at conferences (also, at no additional charge). I have never been treated by a traditional doctor who has provided this type of care. He is dedicated to the care of his patients and is invested in their health. He does research and knows my medical history very well, so he is careful with his recommendations. That is the most reassuring thing when everything feels so medically fragile. He is worth every penny.

Massage:

It's not just for the wealthy. With a little research, I was able to locate two local massage clinics by professional masseuses that charged $35 for an hour session. And they were by far the best massages I have ever had! Massage helps with stress, digestion, headaches, tension, lymph drainage, and promotes healing and sleep. Do your own research or ask Facebook, because it's definitely a worthwhile experience to invest in.

Lemon Balm:

What a game-changer here, folks! For years, people told me about lemon balm, but I shrugged it off, thinking what I was dealing with was way beyond curing with some tincture. I was a convert from day one. It made me feel calmer and clearer-minded. I cannot recommend this product enough. Any natural food store, vitamin store, or Amazon should carry this.

Traditional Medicine:

I need thyroid replacement medication to stay alive since my thyroid was removed. So I am very grateful for Tirosint, a pure version of synthetic thyroid medication. But I have struggled for so many years to take traditional medicine. My body tends to overreact to medicine, and I usually end up with the side effects that only 1% of people get. Yay me. So I avoided traditional medicine even to my detriment. Folks, I am all for natural, but we need to have balance and know when to say "uncle." Yes, I try yoga before I take Tylenol for a headache, but if you are panicking and you need a Xanax, ummm, "take a little wine for your stomach sake" (1 Timothy 5:23). God also created this medicine, along with other traditional anxiety and depression medications. Do the work of counseling, exercise, self-care and eating right, but it is never failure or ungodly because you have to use medication for a season to help your body. This same principle goes with so many other medicines. Do your part, but then also accept the life vest that is being thrown to you.

Turmeric Water:

Turmeric is nature's most potent anti-inflammatory. I did liquid turmeric in my water multiple times a day. With most autoimmune disorders, there is an element of inflammation that causes irritation and pain. So this significantly helps combat that. Plus, it helps spice up plain water, which is not terrible.

Yoga:

Although counterintuitive to a body in pain, movement is often one of the first recommendations from physicians. I knew I was not going to be training for a marathon. I did not have the energy or strength. But I wanted to move. A therapist recommended I check out yin yoga. A gentle, slow yoga where you hold poses for two-to-five minutes at a time. You must focus on the breath and the movement and not your thoughts. It was a wonderful time of movement meditation. If you are thinking, "I don't have money for that," well neither did I. I looked up YouTube practices. You don't even need a mat if you have some carpet in your house. From there, I discovered Yoga with Adriene, a YouTube yogi who I did not want to punch in the face. I cannot stress to you enough how awesome her guided practices are. Please, do yourself a favor and check her out. There is yoga for anxiety, headaches, stress, depression, and so on.

For the longest time, I only felt pain-free while on the mat, mind disengaged from the pain and anxiety, but focused on movement and breathing. I became more flexible and stronger, both emotionally and physically. I will be a yogi for the rest of my life.

Do not be discouraged or overwhelmed because you have not tried "all the things," or because this list feels like a mountain you cannot climb right now. You are not required to, and your personality and journey are unique to you. This is not a guilt list. This is a record of things that have helped. May they help you or you give them a "and a good day to you sir" salute. Whichever way you choose, Namaste.

When Life Goes On

I am writing this chapter while the wee one is in her parkour/martial arts/gymnastics class. She is typically only one of a few girls while she climbs the massive rope and jumps off of mats that are three times her height. She is so brave. She also does all of this with fifteen clips in her hair because "she can do it herself" and wears her ballet tutu. It's precious. This is the only time today I have been able to squeeze in writing. My day job as a designer, followed by household chores, errands, and maintenance, has taken up every spare minute I have. Also, I am having a flare-up. It's great timing as I recently launched this new business, and I am also going on a mini-vacation with my family for four days. If you are thinking, well that will at least mean a nice time to relax, please envision thirteen people (seven of them kids) in a 900-square-foot rental with two bedrooms and one bathroom. Yeah, do that math. Not the sliced cucumbers on my eyes with a lemonade I was imagining. The bottom line is this: Your disease or flare-up is not on your time. It is rarely convenient. But life continues to happen. Day and night are still occurring, and people are still believing the earth is flat. Life goes on. So how do we best adapt to this never-ending cycle?

First, for me, I came to realize that my "best" is temperamental and situational. My "best" when my child has a cold, my new dog is still not potty trained, and I am having a flare-up, looks much different than the kind of morning where it feels like a reenactment of a scene out of Cinderella and the mice bring me my clothes and the birds sing to me. Grace must become the virtue by which we live our lives, both for us and our loved ones. We may not always be on our top game. As a matter of fact, we don't need to be. The greatest gift we can provide our children is resilience, which is achieved through failure and the rise from it. Show your children and mate your A-game and F-game. Apologize liberally, but never for being sick. This creates better humans than perfection ever has.

Second, you must also look for solutions, not the problems. That sixty-hour-a-week stressful job you have may need to be re-evaluated. This, of course, may interfere with your standard of living. So you may need to make a new budget or adjust your spending. These may seem like problems at first. But the more stress you allow in your life, the worse you're going to feel. This is universal of all chronic illness. Stress is NOT your friend. You have a choice: stress and sickness, OR, change and life. You cannot have both. Not anymore.

This may come across as harsh, but I assure you, it is not. It is out of love. Because I did not listen to this advice when I first got sick. I decided I could be a newly adoptive mother and work long hours as a child abuse attorney. I was stressed to the max, but chained to my identity. I had gone to law school, focusing on child abuse law. I passed the freaking bar exam and developed expertise in a very niche area of law. If I left this field, I would have to learn an entirely different area of law, and nothing else really jumped out to me. So I stayed in the field. When things got bad, I decided to leave, but really there was not much of a choice. I was frequently in doctors' offices and hospitals. I had to spend a whole year out of work before I could even consider working again. I had pushed things too far because I focused on the problem, not the solution.

I can tell you I have had more than I could ever dream, and have also lived in a single bedroom in my parents' house with a husband, toddler, and an eighty-pound Flat-Coated Retriever, all while a grown adult. And contrary to my childhood fantasy that if I drove a BMW, had a hot husband, a beautiful house, and a prestigious title, I would be happy, it is, unfortunately, a big fat lie. I was just as happy living in my parents' home. Why? Because happiness and gratitude are heart issues, not money issues. Your standard of living may change, but your happiness does not have to. That is also a choice you will get to make.

Third, you take the time you need to do the things that refresh your soul. You do not apologize for any time needed to regroup. Your kids will be fine. Your husband will be fine. You go drive around your neighborhood with the windows down while blasting your favorite jams and simultaneously crying (not that I have done that). You make room for friendships. You meditate and seek wise counsel. You do the things that bring you back to your whole. However, you need to fit it in.

Need some solutions?

If you have kids:

- Child-swap with a girlfriend, where she watches your kid for a couple hours, and then you watch hers.
- Give your child independent living skills by teaching them how to cook basic meals and have them prepare a meal once a week.
- Do a chore chart with your kids and tie it back to how much screen time they will earn that day. You might initially get some flack, but one day without a phone or TV should do the trick. If you have little ones, teaching them "mommy is not a maid" should start early for their personal growth and your sanity.

- Enroll your child in a learning program or get a babysitter or nanny. This is not failure as a parent, this is choosing how to be the best parent you can be. Rest and downtime are necessities for everyone, but especially someone with chronic illness.
- Find activities to do with your child that are beneficial for both of you. You do not have to be the clown for your kids' entertainment all the time. Being a good parent has nothing, and I mean nothing, to do with how long you can play chase or Mommy Monster with your kids. Kids need more rest and less stimulus in this 24/7 high-impact world. Coloring, painting, chalk art, painting rocks, puzzles, bubbles, and reading books are all low-energy activities with high impact. Connection with your children is what you are after, not their entertainment.

Solutions for married folks:

- Day dates are always a go-to for me because I am usually much more tired at night.
- If you are struggling with your sex life: Scheduling sex does not feel sexy. However, happily married couples often do, because, you know, life. And we are not living in a Rom-Com. Have a conversation with your mate about his needs. How often does he need sex? See if that is a reasonable number for you. If not, compromise. It's about the needs of both of you. Pity sex is usually not the most fulfilling sex. So if your husband says he needs sex twice a week, and that works for you, then go with that. You don't have to chart it out. Let your sex life still be as organic as possible. But I would recommend you cuddle and kiss every single night. It does not have to end in sex, and make that very clear to your spouse. It is just to

ensure intimacy is still flowing, and it makes having sex a smoother transition because the physical affection is still there.
- Easy Going Date Nights, even if you're having a flare-up:
  - Strolling through a local garden. Bringing a thermos full of hot chocolate or wine and solo cups.
  - Candlelit dinners of pizza in bed with a good Rom-Com.
  - Getting a special treat and sitting by a lake.
  - Hanging on the back porch of a trusted friend with wine and whine.
  - Getting crazy dressed up like the Great Gatsby and have a picnic in the park.

You don't have to give up on things that bring you joy even if they tend to stress the body. You just need to practice moderation with them. I am a full believer in the healing power of laughter and joy. So if a particular activity brings you that, keep doing it.

There is always a solution. There is always a way. Sometimes you must actively seek it; other times, you get smacked in the face with it. The important thing is that you continue to dream, hope, play your roles, and live. Oh, girl, really live. Live in ways you never thought you would. Love in ways you never thought your heart had space for. Open up your eyes and arms with compassion. Trust God with reckless abandon, knowing He will never let you down. He will always be the support you need. He will always have your back and the next play ready. He will be your constant guide. He will be your greatest companion, truest friend, and secret keeper. He will make all things good in His time. He will work everything out in your favor. He will give you His strength when you have run out of yours. He will sustain you in your worst days and cheerlead you on in your best. He won't ever give up.

Life will go on. You will find ways to thrive in the ebbs and flows. You will. I promise. That is why it is so important to fill your heart and time with the things that bring you clarity and joy. That's why I am typing with a computer on my lap while I sit in a gym that smells like feet. May you find your moments, and may they smell better than mine.

What Do I Write?

I am at the beginning of what feels like a dip in my system. The first sign of rain. Hormonally things just feel... off. I hate it. It started with a pain-filled moment as I dropped my little one off at her school program. A new sensation I had never felt before. The panic pricked its ears up. "What's going on here? I think I should sound the alarm," it bellowed. I jumped into action as I have learned to do. "No fear, you are just a classic overreactor, and we are not dying nor need to go to the hospital. Let's just let this be and see how it plays out, but I am going to need you to take a hot bowl of cool your jets, right now." It helps. I am grateful now to be in a place where the self-talk is potent and bring things back down. But it has left me feeling, well, defeated. The familiar talk and questions and accusations want to come play. "How long must I deal with this God? I have been so good lately, look, I am even writing a book. How about a little quid pro quo here?" This turns into the self-flagellation of "Get it together woman! You are writing a book here. God is not punishing you, and if you just had more faith, you wouldn't go there." I still go a few rounds with these foes. You know why? Because I am still a human. Because pain hurts. Because even though I have come to fully believe God's way is better and my life is more amazing than I could have imagined it, I still don't want to be sick.

Sometimes I want what God can give me way more than I want God. And He gets that. I avoided writing today because I did not know what to write. I felt hypocritical and sad. How do I tell people to trust God when they are dealing with hardship when I still doubt? But you know what? Abraham doubted God would give him a child as He promised, so he took matters into his own hands. An action that has so significantly changed history it still now effects the Middle East. Gideon was told to lead an army. Moses was told to lead the nation of Israel out of slavery. God appeared to these men in physical form and showed them signs and miracles, and they still said, "Sorry, wrong guy." Thomas was in the original posse of Jesus. He spent day and night with this man for three years. He heard Jesus say with His own mouth, "I will die and in three days be raised to life again," and Thomas still said, "I will not believe Jesus is alive unless I stick my hand in his side" (John 20). Brazy.

And even though he doubted, Abraham was still given that promised son whose ultimate heritage resulted in Jesus' birth. Even though he doubted, Moses led the people out of slavery and was called "the friend of God." Even though he doubted, Gideon defeated a great nation with only three hundred men, some trumpets, and pots. Even though he doubted, Thomas went out into the world and gave hope to many people.

We are not less than or unusable because we doubt. God knows we are human. He knows we are self-centered and focused. He knows we often come to Him because we want something. He even knows that we usually will start with praise just so we can butter Him up. And yet He still wants to prove His faithfulness and His trustworthiness to us! "The fear of the Lord is the beginning of wisdom" (Proverbs 9:10 NIV). Fear here is not in the trembling sense, it's deference. The respectful movements of one who doesn't know the way. In deference to the ways of the Lord, I do not run ahead. I take each step at a time while looking to the One leading the way. This is trust. This is how trust is built. If I follow you and we end up lost, I am going to think twice before retaking your directions. But God has never once lead me astray. Never. Sadly, this is an exercise I do in hindsight because I have often felt confused by the path as I am on it.

So I write to you in honesty. I still doubt. This is still hard. I still wallow sometimes. I still struggle with counting this all joy (James 1:2 NIV). But I know my God is with me. So I cry, and then I tell myself the truth. I will get through this. I will see the other side of this. God will give me everything I need. I write the words "trust and everything" on my hands. I claim His promise that "when I go through the waters, he will be with me; and when I go through the rivers, they will not overwhelm me" (Isaiah 43:3 NIV). I remember that my God has never failed me. So I pray, Lord, help my unbelief, and I hold on.

Who You Are

I believe that Trauma Brain is a commonly overlooked occurrence in people with autoimmune conditions and chronic illness. The disease itself so alters our lives that it, in turn, changes our brains. A little science lesson here. We have three control centers in our brain: The Thinking Center (Pre-Frontal Cortex), the Emotional Regulation Center (Anterior Cingulate Cortex), and Fear Center (Amygdala). The Thinking Center controls personality, problem solving, and rationality. The Emotional Regulation Center does just that, regulates emotions. It gives you that second thought before you do something reckless like giving your boss the middle finger after she says you have to work the weekend. The Fear Center is responsible for your response to stressful stimuli: your Fight-Flight-Freeze-Faint reactions. These are responses beyond your conscious control. They can be very helpful if you are being chased by a bear (well, I guess it wouldn't be awesome if you fainted, unless you encounter a grizzly). But overall, this is a valuable asset to protect you. The problem comes in when the proportions of these Centers become skewed. The Fear Center can become overly fat and hyperactive. You may over-respond to a simple disagreement with your husband. You may feel too emotional and like you cannot control your responses well. You may not even remember specific events or have hazy memories. You may become fearful to do everyday activities that used to not bother you. You may want to calm down and may not be consciously processing an event, but your body is still hypervigilant and experiencing higher heart rates. You may have brain fog, inability or difficulty in concentrating, problems sleeping or calming down, chronic stress, and irritation. This is Trauma Brain.

I lived in a world where you had to earn your Trauma Brain. I had all of the above symptoms, but since I had never been a soldier in Iraq, I reasoned I could not have Trauma Brain. I denied it. I saw myself as weak for not being able to handle things better. But getting sick was my own Iraq. I do not say this to belittle anything soldiers have endured. What I am saying is that the body will have its response regardless of what you may think is or is not justified, and you can either embrace this and try to curb it early, or you can take a trip down the emotional rabbit hole.

When I finally acknowledged my Trauma Brain, things did not immediately get better. Healing takes time. But knowing there was a reason for these responses did make it easier. Relief that I was not actually out of control or irretrievably broken. It was one step at a time, and one truth at a time that finally landed me on the right road to whole. Also, identifying my triggers was so very helpful. My triggers were doctor's appointments and new physical sensations. My body would go numb, waiting for the trigger to subside. To combat this, I would bring my husband to all appointments so there would be someone coherent to hear what the doctor was saying, and I would speak truth over myself. Affirmations became an integral part of my emotional recovery and physical wellbeing. But there would be times when I could not think of a single positive thing to remind myself; because let's be honest, gratitude is not the thing that Trauma Brain goes to first. So I began with these affirmations:

- I am enough. Right now. As I am. Always.
- God loves me.
- I am seen.
- This is not the end.

- I have self-control.
- I have everything I need to succeed.
- I have a strong mind.
- I am a badass.
- I am stronger than I know.
- I am powerful.
- I am full of love.
- I am filled with the divine.
- I am a child of the Most High.
- The God of Angel Armies will fight for me.
- I will thrive here, not just survive.
- I am a good wife/mom/friend/daughter.
- This is a new and good beginning.
- I am doing the best I can.
- I am becoming my truest self.
- I will see the goodness of the Lord in this lifetime.
- God will restore the broken years.
- I am capable of handling this.
- I can do all this because God gives me strength.
- I get to choose my emotions.
- I declare that I am calm and peaceful.
- I will grow here.
- I am not a victim.
- I am victorious.
- I know God has a good plan for me in this.
- I can overcome fear.
- The truth will set me free.
- I will choose trust.
- I will think of things that are good, lovely and true.
- I will also get a good measure of the good times of God's healing comfort.
- God will give me a garment of joy for a cloak of heaviness.

- There is perfect peace for those whose minds are fixed on Jesus.
- There is no fear in love.
- Though I may have stumbled, I will not fall.
- I am not alone.
- This can only end in redemption, love, mercy, grace, and hope.

You are not Trauma Brain. It is just a warning sign that is leading you to healing. You are all of these affirmations and more. I hope you come back to this list and read it over and over again. Better yet, I hope you build on this list and write it all over the place to remind yourself. You don't have to feel it, just choose to believe it. The healing is coming.

What's Your Iceberg?

Thanks to the Titanic, I think we all know an iceberg's mass is ninety percent below the surface. We also know two people could have fit on the door, Rose, but I digress. Moral of the story: It's often what you don't see that will sink your ship.

I had initially gone into EMDR therapy because I was getting overly anxious when I went to doctor's appointments. It was over six months before we even discussed that point. Because for me, it wasn't ever about the doctors, it was about feeling out of control. Control is my iceberg.

When I find I am becoming overly anxious about anything, if I begin to break it down piece by piece, it will inevitably lead me back to an inner child who feels entirely out of control and so in response, my body sounds the alarm to anything that even feels remotely foreign or dangerous, because then we would be out of control, and we could not possibly allow that.

Bottom Line: If you are battling with depression, sadness, anxiety, fear, emotional instability (I don't care what you call it), you, my dear, have an iceberg. You have a surface manifestation of something far deeper within you.

Often, that source hales from childhood. It could be something benign; it does not have to be altogether stereotypically traumatic or tragic, just something that created a system of belief. A few of the common reoccurring culprits are as follows: perfectionism, people-pleasing, control, rejection, shame, fear, bitterness. This is, of course, not an exhaustive list, just the ones I have noticed over the years in myself and others. But hear this: You will never conquer your emotions and bring them under self-control as God has given you the power to do if you do not unearth your iceberg. You may not have to do it sitting in a therapist's office, but one way or another, the whole thing must be turned upside down before the real healing in your soul can truly begin.

Do not be scared of your iceberg. Often we want to just leave the past in the past, and we genuinely think we do, until that past won't leave us, and it manifests in unhealthy ways in our present. Then we are forced to face it. But memories are just that; they are not new things you will have to experience. You have already lived through them. To some degree, the worst is done. This is not new trauma; this is just a puzzle starting to fit together. If anything, it will bring more order to the picture, as opposed to trying to complete the puzzle upside down.

So be brave enough to go there. Ask your soul the tough question of "why?" Allow the Holy Spirit to open your eyes to the depths and then be even braver and allow the Holy Spirit to be the one to heal you. Seek wise counsel. Seek therapy. Seek God. You will find your answers. It will not remain hidden for long. But remember, once you find your answer, you are not responsible for the change and healing. That is God. You are responsible for taking every thought captive and surrendering all the pain to the One who can melt that iceberg and make you whole again.

This will be worth it. This is worth it. For you, for them. For healing. Your ship does not have to sink.

On Dens and Fire

The book of Daniel contains some fantastic stories of trust and deliverance. It's easy to think Daniel and his friends were larger than life characters. Like they had some supernatural ability to trust God. In all actuality, their life circumstances should have made them pretty bitter with God. These boys were of the royal family. Raised with privilege and luxury, and then one day their homes were destroyed by a fierce army who came to pillage and destroy. Most likely, their families were killed. Then they were captured and stripped down. They were made into eunuchs (if you don't know how that process works, please, I implore you to not Google it). Let's just say they were left without the possibility of procreation. They were then forced to work as slaves. That's a hell of a lot a trauma. Therapy for days needed here. The Babylonian King decides he wants to take some of these prisoners of war and train them to become good Babylonians. He assigns the boys particular food and drink from the King's own table. But the boys refuse the spoils and request water and vegetables instead, per Levitical Law. The warden of the boys is worried they will end up being malnourished and his head will roll for it. But Daniel requests ten days of this diet and trusts God will bless him and his friends for keeping the law. Lo and behold, at the end of ten days, they are radiating health and wellness like Gisele Bundchen at the MET ball.

Because of their faithfulness, God, in turn, blesses them by giving them "knowledge and understanding of all kinds of literature and learning and to Daniel specifically, he gave the ability to understand visions and dreams of all kinds" (Daniel 1:17 NIV). With these gifts, they were able to win over the admiration and respect of their captors and achieve high positions within the kingdom. Their positions of esteem go on to dictate the course of history and kingdoms as they advised the highest powers in the known world.

Daniel is so beloved that the King intends to place him as the second-highest in the Kingdom. But the jealous-mac-jealous-pantsers intend to find fault with Daniel so they can dethrone him. They appeal to the King's vanity and say, "Issue a decree that for thirty days, everyone must only pray to you. And if someone violates the law, they will be thrown into the lions' den." The King is super prideful, so clearly he likes this idea, and says, "Why the heck not? Let's do this!" Unfortunately, the King has zero foresight, and the law of the land forbids any edict to be repealed. Daniel hears about the decree, understands the consequences, and then gets on his knees and prays.

I don't think this was an act of defiance. I think this was an act of desperation. Of course, Daniel was scared. He did not want to be eaten by lions, for heaven's sake. So with shaking knees, he hit the floor, and he prayed "just as he had done before" (Daniel 6:10 NIV). I am sure Daniel's prayers were a little different that day, more in the vein of "Save me, God, I don't want to be eaten." But Daniel was still thrown into the lions' den. He had to stay there all night. But ultimately, God had heard Daniel and answered his prayers by shutting the mouths of the lions, which saved Daniel from death.

Then you have Daniel's friends. Different King. Same pride issue. The new King passes an edict that says at the sound of music everyone must bow to the golden image he set up, and if you don't, you will be thrown into a furnace. So the music plays, the friends keep standing, the tattletales go to the King. The boys say they will not bow and believe their God will save them. The King's ego is bruised, and the boys are thrown into the fiery furnace. But God... He shows up in the fire with them, and they are all walking around like it's a casual mixer at a garden party. The King calls the boys out of the flames, and there is not a blister anywhere. They don't even smell like smoke!

I'm not sure if the boys thought this was the way it would go down. I think they were hoping to not enter the flames at all. God answered Daniel's prayers, but probably not in the way Daniel was imagining. You think Daniel wanted to spend the night in a den full of hungry lions?! As members of the royal family of Israel, I am sure the boys thought they would achieve positions of great respect in their lives, but I don't think they thought it would come at the cost of the death and destruction of their families and manhood. I think, as humans, we would like to avoid as much fear and pain as possible. But God still allows us to be in places of fear. Don't misunderstand this. God was not causing these things to happen. God is pro-choice, and so He allows people to make decisions, even ones that are wrong, bad, or evil. Because God values relationships, and a forced relationship is abusive. We can't want free will and then complain when bad things happen. We are not being puppeted. You picking up what I am putting down? But God will absolutely show up in our decisions willfully or forcibly made against us, and He will help us. That does not mean God will always save us from the pain or feelings of fear. Often times, it is the opposite. This is not because God is cruel. It is because the world is cruel, and God is giving us the greatest gifts of all: resilience, strength, compassion, empathy, and love.

So we may have to sit in our dens or walk through the fires. Our knees may shake, and our hands tremble, but God promises us this: "When you walk through the fire, you will not be scorched; the flames will not set you ablaze" (Isaiah 43:3 NIV). The intention in life is not to be fearless. Fear is a good thing. It keeps us safe. It is when it consumes us and lies to us that it becomes toxic. God promises to walk with us when we walk through the storms of life. He promises His everlasting arms and presence. We have the luxury of hindsight into these men's stories, but they had no clue how this was going to play out in their lives. But in the face of their fears and pain, they chose to trust. They chose obedience. And God did not disappoint.

We often miss blessings because they are not what we expected. We want the deliverance to look different. We don't want to feel pain and fear at all, so we believe anything short of that is not salvation, is not the miracle. But these men walked out of their doom with salvation AND a deeper trust in God and MORE strength. Don't short-change yourself and God. Get it all.

Oh, That Healing

I am a massive fan of *The Princess Bride*. I think I may be able to quote the entire movie. One of my favorite scenes is where Fezzik and Inigo Montoya are storming the castle to free Princess Buttercup from the evil Prince Humperdinck. The Gatekeeper is denying that he has the keys to the gate, and Inigo says to the Giant Fezzik, "Tear his arms off," to which the Gatekeeper responds, "Oh, you mean this gate key?"[8] If this is a spoiler alert to you, get over it. The statute of limitations has passed, and I can now quote this movie with reckless abandon.

In the introduction, I address this one little time where God promised He would heal me. But then I wrote this book about God and chronic illness and clearly am still struggling with the topic. So what the heck is that about? Did God lie? Is He just waiting for some arbitrary time in history to do what He said he would? Did I just make it up in my mind because that is what I wanted to hear?

I have wrestled with these questions so many times. Here are my conclusions on "that healing," waiting and hearing.

God does not lie. Satan is the author of all lies, and there is no good in him. God would never mislead me. I have at times bit on the lie that God is like a horoscope that reads, "Something good will happen today," and we want to believe it so badly we justify it and make it the truth. "Yes, I started a flare-up, my daughter got the flu and my new puppy pissed on my bed, but I did have a good hair day. Thanks, horoscope." It's a self-fulfilling prophecy. God works in ways I cannot. He knows things I should not. He sees things I will not. So His fulfillment of promises often looks different than my expectations. But I do not serve the magic genie of the lamp, and like a good parent, He gives us what we need, not what we always want. So God's promises are not horoscope fodder. Satan desperately wants us to believe they are, so we doubt God and mistrust ourselves and our ability to hear God. What would be a better strategy than to get us to second guess everything so we remain immobile? Here is a good litmus test for all times when you are confused: "Does this bring me closer to God, or is this driving me from Him, whether by guilt, shame or doubt?" If the later, it's not from God.

God does not purposefully hide Himself or good things from us. He is not looking for me to be good enough, loving enough, giving enough, or clean enough to then heal me. His timing is ultimately perfect. But the wait can, well, suck. There have been many times in my life, and I am sure yours, if you think back, where you could say, "I finally understood what that meant." It is usually not a novel idea, but because of your maturity and position in life, the concept finally clicked. The same goes for God's timing. There is a perfect time, a place where it all clicks, and the wait makes sense.

God does something very beautiful for us, He confirms His word. He does this through:

1. The Bible,
2. Prayer,
3. The Holy Spirit moving within us with His still small voice and,
4. Other people.

If God reveals something to you, and you feel unsure, you better believe God will double down on His word by the means above. He understands doubt, and He is not a one-and-done God.

Oh, That Healing

"Oh, you did not hear that still small voice, I guess you ruined my plans for your life." Nonsense. God is not petty. God did confirm my healing through my lovely pastor friend, and I am so grateful. I am sure if I did not receive the confirmation through her, I would have lost trust in the process a long time ago.

But here is the thing: I may never be without flare-ups. I may have rest days and smoothie-only days. This healing may be a whole lot more than healing my body. But I do know He is healing my mind. He is bringing me closer to the person I always wanted to be. Richard Rohr addressed this idea of the truest self in his book *Falling Upward*: In life, you will have pain and crises, but it does not have to end there. The crisis can define your life, but if you are open to it, you can instead use it as a catalyst to enter a place of spiritual revival, love, peace, and empathy that you could not have imagined before.[9] No truer words.

I have grown in my pain. I have come to understand the toxicity of perfectionism, the embracement of bravery, the desire for deeper empathy and compassion, the equality of all beings. These changes, in and of themselves, are miracles and such a juxtaposition from my lofty, black-and-white heart before my diagnosis. These are paradigm shifts I would not have discovered sans health crisis. And so they are a healing.

But if I am to be transparent, of course, I hope my healing includes physical symptoms. But I cannot let my expectations of God drive my relationship with Him. If my obedience is solely based on hopes that one day He will physically heal me, then it is no relationship at all. The issue is the heart condition here. Will I be okay if God never physically heals me? It took a long time for me to come to this conclusion, but yes, I will be okay. I am so grateful for the person I am becoming by the healing in my heart. I am getting closer and closer to my truest self. The person I like with or without flare-ups. It is becoming well with my soul.

And Only Sometimes Let Your Conscience Be Your Guide

Call it what you want: conscience, sixth sense, gut feeling, third eye, Jiminy Cricket, or inner critic. We all have something within us that guides us. But it is crucial to test the fruit of that internal guide. Richard Rohr writes of this in *Falling Upward*, where we all have a loyal soldier within us that directs our lives. He uses this analogy because of a sacred ceremony that occurred in Japan after WWII. The soldiers were coming home from battle, and many were having difficulty acclimating back into civilian life. So the Japanese developed a day of recognition and high praise for the sacrifices these soldiers made for their country. When the praise ceased, they were provided civilian clothes and asked to enter a new stage in life. A beautiful rebirth.[10]

For most of us, the internal, loyal soldier keeps us in line and out of jail. It bullies us into good behavior. It can be motivated by things like achievement, pride, self-protection. Not all bad things, necessarily. It wants to see us succeed and keep us out of hot water. But often that loyal soldier can be misconstrued for the voice of God, and there is no room for compassion, mercy, and love there.

My loyal soldier was a real jerk. It left me isolated from others, claiming to be "set apart." It made me judgmental and prideful. It caused me to see perfectionism as a legitimate way of living. It made me effective, but joyless. It disallowed any bravery and chance-taking. It kept me confined and safe. It, in fact, did keep me out of physical jail, but it imprisoned my heart.

I was done with chains. I wanted freedom. So, I quietly thanked my loyal soldier for her service and then asked her to step aside, so I could enter this new life. As a good soldier does, she has fought back on multiple occasions. I have gone through periods of time when I have not heard from her, not even a call. But then I try something very daring, and she starts calling like a jilted girlfriend who just went through her philandering boyfriend's texts. So I call her out and look her in the face and tell her, "I am going on this journey with or without you." And I walk forward, sometimes with my knees shaking and trembling hands, but forward.

Does your loyal soldier allow room for grace, mercy, and love? Does she speak kindly to you and lead you to peace and wholeness? If she does not, this is not the voice of God. If she resorts to guilt and shame tactics to correct behavior, this is not the Holy Spirit. It's your inner critic. Your loyal soldier. Discharge them. Claim your freedom, and walk toward your victory. They may come along, but never, ever let them drive.

Be a Betsy

Corrie Tenboom writes about her sister, Betsy, in her book *The Hiding Place*.[11] They were in a concentration camp during WWII, and the whole place was infested with fleas. Betsy tells Corrie to be thankful for the fleas because the guards do not enter the barracks because of them, and that gives Corrie and Betsy time to tell people about Jesus. I am not sure I could ever reach Betsy Tenboom's level, but I wanted to try. So I convinced my girlfriends to go on a negative word faste and to group text each other daily about what we were grateful for that day. On day two, my girlfriend was having a crappy day getting prenatal work-ups and venting on a group text, but then she wrote, "So to be thankful for the fleas, I am thankful for quiet time alone, my book to read and bills to pay in peace." This clearly is no concentration camp situation, but we can get so caught up in the fleas that we fail to see the blessings in front of us. Can you imagine how this new mindset would change our lives? Our relationships with our families and friends? Mates and kids? How much physically better we would feel because we have chosen to not allow the toxicity of the day to be the final word?

In the beginning, when I got a lot of questions about my diagnosis, I would feel a tension rise in my throat, and sometimes it even hurt to speak. I vacillated from wanting to wear a t-shirt that said, "Hi, I have Chronic Illness. Be nice," and pretending this never happened. This diagnosis was a juncture in my life. I refer to these as B.C. and A.D. moments. Like the timeline markers of Before Christ and Anno Domini. There was life before this moment, and then there was life after this moment. Fear started to take hold right from the beginning. How long will I deal with this? Will this get worse? When will I have another flare-up? I have to perform. How can I perform? I need to hide this because people do not understand. And on and on the fear cycle spun.

In turn, this made every good moment a matter of foreboding joy. The great Brene Brown spoke of this when she stated, "If you ask me what's the most terrifying, difficult emotion we feel as humans, I would say joy…How many of you have ever sat up and thought, 'Wow, work's going good, good relationship with my partner, parents seem to be doing okay. Holy crap. Something bad's going to happen…' You know what that is? [It's] when we lose our tolerance for vulnerability. Joy becomes foreboding: 'I'm scared it's going to be taken away. The other shoe's going to drop…' What we do in moments of joyfulness is, we try to beat vulnerability to the punch."[12] Namaste, Brene Brown. You are so right.

If you perpetually live your life in fear of the other shoe dropping, well guess what, all you are going to see is a lot of shoes on the ground. You will never see the wildflowers growing through the sidewalk. Because though "we have plenty of hard times that come from following [Jesus] [we] have no more so than the good times of his healing comfort – we get a full measure of that too" (2 Corinthians 1:5 NIV). Yeah, this life sucks terribly sometimes. But it also is so full of goodness and beauty and love and miracles and grace and forgiveness. I want you to think about five awesome things right now. I am not kidding, dog-ear this book and stop and think about five things you love. This is where we have to start. Gratitude. Thankfulness. We never start with happiness. That is a byproduct of a heart full of gratitude. We do not get there without the cornerstone.

You have the power to control your thoughts. You and Aunt Flow[13] may not believe that, but you really do. God says it right here: "God has not given you a spirit of fear. But one of power, love, and SELF-CONTROL" (2 Timothy 1:7 ESV). It may be hard to feel the self-control because of years of lack of self-discipline. But that wild horse of a mind can be tamed. It just takes a bit of time and practice, and here is the best part: It's not all on you. God will help you and give you the tools you need. It's not some eloquent prayer, although I am not knocking that, I am just saying you don't have to be C.S. Lewis to get God to answer your prayer. A simple: "Jesus help me" is sufficient. Read books by amazing women of faith like Beth Moore and Priscilla Shirer. Listen to praise music. Here's my plug again for anything by Steffany Gretzinger. Copy and paste scriptures into the notes section of your phone and read them while you are at a stoplight. Stop watching *Game of Thrones* and fill your mind with "whatever is true, whatever is noble, whatever is right, whatever is pure, whatever is lovely, whatever is admirable—if anything is excellent or praiseworthy—think about such things" (Philippians 4:8 NIV). Get all *A Beautiful Mind* on yourself and write inspirational and loving words of God on your bathroom mirror. Feed the light within you with beauty and truth over and over again, and it will start to come flowing out of you with ease. And I promise, if you do these things, you will feel lighter and freer. Don't feel overwhelmed by this. I know I did at first when these things were mentioned to me. It will not always have to be at this level. And I am not saying to cancel your subscription to Netflix and only listen to Christian music. God knows I love me some Beyoncé. You just may need to fill yourself more fully with other things for a season until the practice of gratitude becomes a habit of gratitude.

I was a classic Debbie Downer. A realist. Sometimes a cynic. I also tended to wallow, and when something good happened to someone I know, I will admit my first thought was, "When is it my turn?" I mean, who wouldn't want to be friends with me?! I didn't like this side to my personality. I wanted to be happy for other people. I wished for once to be described as "bubbly," not Resting Belle (or a more colorful word) Face. I thought this was my personality, and so I needed to just embrace it. Listen, your personality is your personality, but a personality flaw is still a flaw. There is a real difference. No one is too old to change. That is a limit we place on ourselves.

I remember telling my husband how much I missed laughing. Like the kind where it hurts your ribs and you pee a little. Chronic illness can be the ultimate kill-joy. And I think I had taken the posture of lost traveler, trying to find my way. This did not lead to many joy-filled life moments. I also did not value or seek feel-good happiness. I found it cheap, and since the higher form of happiness is intrinsic happiness, that is the one I solely focused on. But the two go hand-in-hand. Light moments of dancing to 1990s jams on the porch with my husband while trying to prove I can do a flip is also worshipping God. He loves fun and joy. He commanded the Israelites to have annual feasts to remember His deliverance and mercies. He loves a good party! So seek both forms of joy. The momentary happiness will fill the soul and put a smile on your face, and the intrinsic happiness will sustain it.

God is very clear in His requirements. Philippians 4:6-7 (ESV) says, "Be anxious for nothing, but in everything by prayer and supplication, with thanksgiving, let your requests be made known to God. And the peace of God, which transcends all understanding, will guard your hearts and your minds in Christ Jesus." I had the prayer part down. As my husband will attest, I have a lot of words, and I directed many of them at God. Lots of requests to stop the pain, heal me, give me strength, give me everything I need. But I was not following the formula. As a person who loves systems, I am surprised by how often I fail to follow this foolproof method of obtaining peace. Asking in Faith + Thanking = Protection of your heart and mind = Peace. I was missing the gratitude. I could barely be happy in the good moments because I was too busy thinking about when the bad moments would return. That foreboding joy again. So I developed a sense of numbness so the highs would not get too high or lows too low. But this self-protection mechanism is not what I wanted either.

The addition of gratitude was the only way I was going to get to where I wanted to go. "In everything give thanks, for this is the will of God in Christ Jesus for you" (1 Thessalonians 5:18 NKJV). Not when things are going right. Not just when your child is acting like a wonderful angel who is very thankful and is sharing all her toys like a saint. Not when your husband offers to give you just a backrub, with his hands. No, nope. In everything, including every flare-up, every Target meltdown (yours or your child's), and every heavy sigh and eye roll from your man. Everything.

Does this make this Debbie happy? Not at all. I like a good wallow. It feels cathartic to witch about your husband and drink too much wine because of your kids. It feels justified given what God has allowed to happen. It is completely in-human to be grateful in these circumstances, and anyone who is happy is a craze. And God agrees. It is inhuman to be thankful in all circumstances because even beyond your diagnosis, the world still sucks sometimes, and really awful things happen. That is where God says: "Try me. Follow the formula. Ask me and thank me in advance, give it all to me, and I will surround your heart and mind with the Angel Armies. I will be the watchman of your mind. I will bring you the peace you are so desperate for. I will always come through. Believe me, and lay it down."

So I started small. Each evening I would write down five things I saw improvement in: "The flare-up was not as painful as before," "I was able to re-regulate my emotions quicker after a stressful event," "I only cried once today." You get the point. It doesn't have to be big things or mountain moving. It is just charting progress and being mindful. Every morning I would write out five things I was grateful for. Starting the day with the mindset on thankfulness as opposed to any pain sensation I may be experiencing is so much better. Even if you are in pain, gratitude is the focus, and it dramatically contributes to the self-talk. This was helpful. But gratitude by itself was not enough for me. I had to believe it. "I am grateful for my kid, husband, house we live in, cute dogs...." It's all nice and good, but if your heart is not in it, it's just fluffery. I realized the benefits of gratitude stem from the roots of belief.

The combination of believing prayer and thankfulness wins every time. I am most thankful for things that have not yet happened. Frequently, thankfulness puts the power behind the prayer. The prayer of "God give me strength" turns into the spoken gratitude of "I thank You in advance, Lord, for the strength I know You will give me." Because I know He will come through. It gives the power punch at the end. You have to believe you are blessed to feel blessed. You have to believe God will come through to really watch for His hand at work. Starting with a gratitude practice will help develop the roots of belief if they are not already there. Taking time to meditate on your blessings is a worthwhile practice that will never turn void. Even when all your brain wants to focus on are the negatives.

I still struggle. I still have to go back to my old strategies when I get bogged down. But each time, it is easier to get back into the rhythm. Gratitude is a muscle that must be exercised to become strong. It will not be overnight. But practice, practice, practice. It will be worth it. Because in a word full of "Debbies," I want to be a "Betsy."

Why Not Me?

God loves to heal. He loves to showcase His glory and miracles so others will trust in Him. God absolutely can heal anyone of anything at anytime. But sometimes, He just does not. I wish I could provide you with the concrete reason why. But the ways of God just will not be known by us this side of heaven. The Bible is clear on this in Romans 11:33 (ESV): "Oh, the depth of the riches and wisdom and knowledge of God! How unsearchable are his judgments and how inscrutable his ways!" It also has nothing to do with God wanting to remain a cosmic mystery and keep us mere mortals in the dark. We don't see His deck of cards for our lives solely for our own good.

If you, before your diagnosis had been given a timeline vision of your life where you realized in a few years you would be diagnosed with a chronic illness, how many of us could have just said: "Eh, let's just make the best out of these next few years." I love me some Tim McGraw and will sing a mean karaoke to "Live Like You Were Dying," but I am not sure I could actually live it. I know I would have worried and pleaded and lost sight of the present because of the impending future. God unrolls things in the right timing and typically does not showcase our lives because He knows our tendency to not live in the present. It's a mercy, not a punishment. So when God chooses to not immediately take this all away, it is also a mercy as well. That may sound sadistic. You may want to shut this book and burn it right now, but hear me out. Your life has never been left up to chance. Everything good or bad in your life has been a beautifully articulated play to grow you, build you, and bless you. God **does not** cause bad things. But He is willing to turn them around for our good because God has loved us with an everlasting love, and has drawn us with unfailing kindness. He will build you up again, and you will be rebuilt (Jeremiah 31:3-4).

The absolute truth is this: God will "never leave you or forsake you" (Deuteronomy 31:6 NIV). He will give you grace this moment, and then the next and then the next. The same goes for His strength and forgiveness. It never runs out. If you ask, it is there. But you must believe it. You must ask in faith. Then, poof, it is yours. We need to stop humanizing God. He is not a friend or a mate who grows weary of your needs or requests. His is the only relationship where dependence is required and healthy. He has never looked at me with annoyance for needing His help again. And He never will.

God does sometimes choose to heal fully or in part, and what an incredible blessing. And for us sometimes perfectionist "Debbies" it can be a real kick in the pants. Because we start to compare our stories with the story of the one who received this blessing. We judge them and ourselves and wonder why we weren't chosen. As if we can somehow earn our healing? Just like the blind man in the Bible or the lepers or the woman who bled for twelve years. They earned their healings by doing amazing acts and giving all their money and, oh wait, no they didn't. They had faith, and Jesus chose to heal them. Not because somehow they were more significant than others, but because it was their destiny to showcase and tell of the miracle God had performed in their lives. The same holds true for those of us who have not been healed yet. We haven't been because God wants us to showcase and tell of all the incredible blessings He has given us IN SPITE of our sickness. The ways we have grown in resilience and strength and compassion. The ways we love deeper and are empathetic to the sufferings of others.

Because people get sick. End of story. And we need victory stories there too. The human spirit needs to hear the triumph over tragedy stories, even more than the miraculous ones because this life is hard, and we need to see others getting through it well, not just holding on. If someone just told you to wait till you are healed, you would never be able to truly live the life you currently have. You would be in a holding pattern, waiting to move forward with a family or career or dream because the healing was coming. But God calls us to prosper even while here. He said to the Israelites that had been carried off as captives: "Build houses and settle down; plant gardens and eat what they produce. Marry and have sons and daughters; find wives for your sons and give your daughters in marriage, so that they too may have sons and daughters. Increase in number there; do not decrease" (Jeremiah 29:5-7 NIV).

Sister, listen to these words, do not decrease here. You don't have to. Do not view yourself or this situation as less than. Do not play the victim. Do not short-change yourself or your family. Change what must be changed, but go forward, daughter of the Most High King. Increase, even here. Especially here, in spite of here. And for Pete's sake, do not mope because someone else's incredible miracle has not been your blessing. You can thrive here too and give amazing amounts of hope to those who are watching your story unfold. "God is close to the brokenhearted" (Psalm 34:18 NIV), and so He is, in fact, actually closer to you and your suffering than those who are walking around without a care in the world.

Here's more hard truth: You don't have to obsess over your health. I am a recovering control addict. Being sick is so difficult for me because it is entirely out of my control. The mind will go crazy playing what my husband and I refer to as "the fun game of why this symptom just happened." What did I do differently? Did I accidentally eat gluten? Did I take my supplements out of order? I would hyper-fixate on trying to find solutions to all of the problems. I tried to control everything I ate and everything I did.

And do you know what that gave me? Not more health if you were wondering. It gave me more anxiety! Yes, take care of your body. It is not a trash can. Use wisdom, be smart. But having a piece of cheese every once in a while is not going to undo you (unless you are lactose intolerant, but you get my point). Balance is better than control. It is better for your mind and for your body. You, in fact, do not have to worry about your health. That is a choice—an attractive one, but nonetheless a toxic one. You do not achieve greater freedom and health the more you try to hold in your hands.

I refused to believe the truth for years. When I first got sick, I became incredibly strict with my diet, and with every subsequent flare-up, something else went out the door. Every new symptom was analyzed and charted, so I could try to prevent it from happening again. All this did was wind me up like a monkey with cymbals, until one day, I was off clanging away. I did not receive the benefit of greater health because I was obsessed with it; I received more stress. The gift that keeps on giving. God cares about your day-to-day health decisions. That is why He provides wisdom and the guidance of the Holy Spirit to provide balance in our lives. These days when a new symptom comes up, I actively say, "I do not need to worry about my health. God has this." It is the only thing that has provided lasting relief. I do not carry this only. And occasionally, I will eat cheese (I know, such a rebel.) Here's the thing: If God chooses not to heal you, then He promises that He will give you everything you need to thrive here (Philippians 4:19). You don't need the promise of healing. You need the Healer. Rest knowing this is His plan. A good one. This is how we thrive in our captivity. This is how we stand tall, look this disease in the eye and say, "Bring it." You've got this, and God has you. Fight on.

The Source of It All

Every good and bad decision can be traced back to one thing: a thought—your mind's initial spark to enter into something destructive or amazing. Everything starts in the mind. With this knowledge, you would assume we would instinctively be careful with what we allow our minds to think. But I guess that would also assume we believe we could, in fact, control our thoughts.

For years I was a passive participant in my thought life. I assumed my thoughts were simply my truths rising up, whether good or bad. I was passive in my response and was overall the victim to whatever horror scenario my mind was cooking up that day. But since the thoughts did not "feel" like they affected my overall health and my physical state of being, I allowed them to come and go carelessly.

That is how it all begins. It's insidious. Small negative thoughts here and there that we let slide. The anger we hold onto, the bad situation we don't seek healing to overcome, the doubts and fears we justify. They all become building blocks for our prison until one day you are diagnosed with anxiety or depression, and you are wondering how you got here and why you can't seem to get out. It all started with a thought that was actually a lie, that we began to accept as truth.

The beautiful thing is that if you can build it, you can also tear it down with the same tools. Thoughts.

- Romans 12:2 (NIV): "Do not conform to the pattern of this world, but be transformed by the renewing of your mind. Then you will be able to test and approve what God's will is - his good, pleasing, and perfect will."
- Philippians 4:8 (NIV): "Whatever is true, whatever is noble, whatever is right, whatever is pure, whatever is lovely, whatever is admirable—if anything is excellent or praiseworthy—think about such things."
- 2 Corinthians 10:5 (NIV): "We demolish arguments and every pretension that sets itself up against the knowledge of God, and we take captive every thought to make it obedient to Christ."

No thought is innocent. Every thought comes with the afterthought of: "Do I believe this is true or not?" The answer to this does not take into account whether the thought actually is true, but whether it feels true. If it feels true, a neural pathway is created or etched deeper. That is why people develop irrational fears, because it was a thought that felt true; therefore, it became a reality in the mind. I don't say this to scare you. If you have one bad thought or one lousy day of thoughts, you are not going to be irretrievably broken with a diagnosable condition. That is not how thoughts work. They take their time. The problem is that Satan also likes to play the long game, and he will work on planting those negative thought seeds so you will never get wise to his game. He is not looking to be seen. He wants you to think they are coming from the most credible source: yourself. But we become wise to this tactic when we evaluate what we allow into our minds. This can be completely tangible as in the things we look at online, on social media, or browsing through our phones. The stuff we binge watch on Netflix or HBO. The things we read or listen to. Are these things positive to your soul? Do they leave you feeling built up and renewed? If they do not, even if you enjoy it, you may need to reconsider its benefit to your life. When the "out of the blue" negative thoughts hit you, are you stern with them? Do you shut them down immediately, or do you go a couple rounds?

You don't have to let the thoughts become feelings, which turn into full-fledged emotions, which become your truth. You have control over your thoughts through the Holy Spirit. You are not a victim of your thoughts. Stop acting like one. You can renew your mind with every thought you think. God is all about this. So He will infuse you with all the strength you need to fight this battle and win. Don't know where to start?

Strategies:

1. Evaluate the content. Is it true? Regardless of feelings, is it ultimately true? I may feel like I am falling apart some days, but am I actually falling apart? No, so I speak to the lie and turn it on its head. "I may feel this way, but I don't have to fear, nor is this my permanent reality. This is a moment."
2. Remember, there is no need to argue with a lie. Simply state: "This is a lie, and I do not pay attention to lies." Done.
3. Spiritually and verbally call it out: "I take every thought captive under the authority of Jesus." You don't have to yell this in the middle of the supermarket. Mouthed, or even under your breath, work just as well. I just feel like there is more authority when I actively open my mouth.
4. Most importantly, replace the negative thought with a gratitude thought. Do NOT skip this step "Debbies." Find your flea moment.

Be patient with yourself in the process. You don't need to add guilt to your thought life when you don't get it right. Because you won't all the time. But it's the recognition of that, and asking for forgiveness from God and others, if need be, and then tapping back into the leading of the Holy Spirit. You will not change on your own. Your own strength will not produce the lasting change you need. Use your spiritual authority so you don't exhaust yourself.

The way you think will become the way you talk and act. Who do you really want to be? Look to the people you admire. Are they the kind of people who griped their way through difficulty and ended up on the other side with bitterness and a side helping of fear? Of course not. We admire the people whose determination of heart and strength of mind brought them through hell, and they did not let it defeat them. This can be your story. You can be the person you admire.

Section Three
Summer

Let's Go Back to Fear

I was told by a very respected infertility doctor I was not able to have a baby. Not only that, but because of the mess of problems between my husband and me, we wouldn't even get pregnant. When your infertility doctor tells you he doesn't want any more of your money and you should probably just go adopt, ummm, you listen. I remember that day so clearly in my mind. I would never have a baby. I would never know what it feels like to have a baby kick from the inside. It was a devastating loss.

I spent years refusing to believe this pronouncement. I denied the infertility and just knew if I was calmer, less stressed, more secure in my faith, healthier…I could get pregnant. I knew God would come through. So I waited. Year one, two, three, four, five. By year six, I couldn't keep the grieving cycle at bay anymore. I needed to get to acceptance. I needed to lay this down. I couldn't keep waiting with bated breath each month only to get a visit from Aunt Flow and then fall apart in a JCPenney bathroom. It was too much. This is not to say my daughter is not amazing or not the answer to my every prayer. Pain from infertility has zero bearing on my absolute love and obsession with her. She is the greatest thing I have ever called mine, and my husband and I say often, "There is no way we could have made a kid cooler than her." She is my dream and my heart. I'm simply saying that infertility sucks, and you have to grieve the loss, even if you hold another child in your arms. That loss has not been replaced.

This is by no means saying lose hope. The act of surrender is not that at all. It is simply saying, "God, I am breaking under the weight of this, and I can't carry this anymore. You are in control. Your way will be best." So I mourned the child I never got to carry. The blue-eyed, blonde-haired little boy I pictured so clearly in my mind. I gave him to God. I asked God to hold me and heal my heart from this deep wound. I looked at the daughter I had with so much more gratitude and love, and finally said in my soul: "This is enough." And I meant it.

Then I got pregnant.

I want to be very clear here. This is not a how-to guide. There is no promise in the Bible that "once you lay it down truly, then you will get pregnant." God is not cruel or unkind, where He plays hide the ball. This is just a story of redemption in my life. If you are struggling with infertility, my heart aches for you. I hope you are encouraged by this story, but do not take this as fact on how God will work in your life as well. I hope He gives you the desires of your heart. I know He will be good. I just don't know how your story is going to turn out. But I know He has a plan that is for your favor. Okay, back to the story.

I was one day late for my period and was about to head on vacation. I tend to overanalyze things and wanted to peacefully go on vacation with a clear mind. So I took an at-home pregnancy test, placed it on the toilet seat, and went to take a shower. I got out of the shower when I realized I had forgotten to throw the test away and didn't want my husband to find the test and think I was neurotic. Because obviously, I was not pregnant. I grabbed the test and went to toss it in the trash, and that is when I noticed the lack of the word "not." I had taken multiple pregnancy tests in the past, always with the same conclusion: "Not Pregnant." I stared at the test and then stared some more. Then walked away, came back, and stared again. "Pregnant."

There were so many ways I had planned to tell my husband I was pregnant. I dreamed up elaborate unfoldings with candlelight and violins, and dedicated songs, and proclamations. But the best I could muster when it finally was a reality was an old mug with a broken handle that read "New Daddy Needs Coffee" and I walked out to our garage where I found him changing the oil in my car, because apparently we are country, and handed him the mug and said: "You're going to need this again."

Y'all, I did not even have brushed teeth or a bra on at this point. This was panic telling. I just couldn't hold this to myself. I would love to say my first response was to burst into songs of praise to God and joyful tears of gratitude. But it was more trembling sobs: part disbelief, part fear, part shock, part happy. How did this happen? I mean, I know how, but HOW??? This was never going to happen. This was not in my cards. This was not in my future. I had made peace with this. And now this?! I was just coming out of a flare-up, did the medicine I had just taken affect the baby? What medicine can I or can I not take now? Am I healthy enough for this? Will this last?

Fear. Leave it to me to turn a miracle into a fear moment. But isn't that just like our enemy? But God...here we are again. I had absolutely nothing to do with this miracle. Honestly, my husband and I had barely exchanged a meaningful glance in the last month due to sickness and schedules. God's hands were all over this, and yet the first thing I wanted to do was take control by fearing. Because that is all it is, a desperate grab for control. But I could not worry my way into the wanted outcome or not. I was not in control. And that is precisely where God started talking.

My devotions in the following days brought me to Job 38 (NIV), God's response to Job's questions. God starts with this line: "Who is this that obscures my plans with words without knowledge?" I used to think God was quite harsh with Job here. I mean, throw him a bone God, the man had lost everything he owns and loves, as well as his health. But these are not the words of an angry God. For the first time, I read these words and was filled with so much comfort. "Who are you? Because I am God." He is in control of this pregnancy. He was the author of it too. I could spend these days scared of a potential loss, or I could spend these days lovingly touching my belly with tears falling down my cheeks in beautiful gratitude for finally being able to experience what my heart had always longed for.

Fear is alluring. It almost feels like the right choice. The expected and approved choice. That's why it is so attractive. But God has good plans for my life. God is so loving. God gave me a precious, incomprehensible miracle. So with everything within me, I will choose praise instead, even if that looks like a bunch of tears and sobs, and then realignment. I will choose gratitude over my fear, mostly because I love God, but also because the alternative sucks and is not really a choice. Because falling apart right now is self-defeating and is not going to lead me to greater trust and health.

So regardless of whether you just found out you were pregnant or not, and if so, Mazel Tov, this chapter is for you because sometimes good ole common sense needs to reign supreme. Yes, we are entering a future that I believe is unprecedented in its approach to emotions and mental health, and it is about damn time too. Telling boys they shouldn't have emotion and to "man up" is archaic and still a lie. Making girls believe they are weak because of their emotions is just stupidly wrong and bad science. I am so glad we are making it past this dark history of sweeping depression and anxiety under the rug. I am glad we are now permitting ourselves not to be okay. I am so happy the global conversation is turning to the embracement of feelings. But, you also have to balance this out with the knowledge that you are strong, that you are not your emotions, and that you can handle strong emotions like an adult.

You can embrace the suck of chronic illness or the fear of finding out you are pregnant after the greatest health battle of your life. You are permitted to stay in that emotional stew without a heck of a lot of judgment from the outside world. You can, go for it. But not a second longer than is needed, and then you dust the dirt off your crown, and you get back on your feet, girl. Stand up. Trust. Walk forward. You don't have to fall apart. The feelings may tell you that you need to, but fleeting feelings are typically filthy liars. Falling apart is honestly not helpful. Because ultimately, and here is the truth: You got this. Because He has you.

I will not fall apart. I will choose faith and trust. I will be okay, no matter what the outcome. Because I am not ultimately in control, and I am putting all my eggs in the basket of the One who is.

The Two Ways

The day I found out I was pregnant, I also developed a cold from hell. I couldn't get out of bed for days. As previously stated, y'all, I don't do rest well, so if I could not muster the wherewithal to get out of bed, you need to understand this was nasty. I was okay emotionally the first five days, but by day six momma was having none of this. I was sick as a dog, nauseous from meds, yet simultaneously pregnant hungry, so that was a treat. I am not fond of over the counter cold medicine as my body tends to over-respond in the "Wow, did she just do drugs?" kind of a way. I certainly was not looking to take medication now, since it is not highly recommended that pregnant women take unnecessary medication. But I could not get better, and so antibiotics and Tylenol Cold and Flu were deemed necessary.

Here we go with the unmet expectations again. I was just trying to wrap my mind around the idea of being pregnant and having to titrate off of medications that had been very helpful for a long time. Then getting sick, then not sleeping for five days straight, then adding in more random and scary medicines…oy vey. It was not the way I thought it would all be. But when it is ever? I was starting to feel those familiar desperate feelings when trust slips, and your prayers begin to feel more like accusations.

It may have been a medication haze, but on day nine God gave me a beautiful vision. As I closed my eyes to try to get some sleep finally, I saw me standing at a floating road with two separate paths laid out before me. To the left was the known: feelings of control, same medications, the same anxiety, same bondage. No pregnancy. To the right was the unknown: a full surrender to God, with only His promises to guide me and see me down the path. But it led to life and peace. "What will you choose?" the vision urged. Did I want to hold onto my faux sense of control more than I wanted the life God promised? Would I literally choose life? I, in no way, wanted to lose this baby, but this baby was an unknown scary element I had no control over. This thought was so sobering. All that week, I had been upset because the path to the left had all of a sudden been blocked, and I wanted my familiar. When all along, the path to life had been laid out, a miracle had been placed inside me, and I was stubbornly refusing to walk down that path because it was the unknown. "God, forgive me," I prayed. "I choose life. I choose to surrender. Help my unbelief."

Sometimes we choose our prison because leaving it would mean vulnerability. It would require strength we do not feel we have inside of us. It would require surrender and the unknown. So we stay because we feel as if we are in control of our prison. It feels safe. But prison is never safe. You absolutely, 100 percent, no doubt about it, can be free from this prison. But you will have to choose life. You will have to choose trust daily. You will have to let God fight for you. You will have to put in the work of studying the truth. You are given the two paths, as well. So what will it be: fear, control, the familiar, safe, OR freedom, surrender, trust, and life? You always get a choice, so choose wisely.

Anger

I thought you would take the anxiety away the moment I claimed your promise of peace. I thought you would stop the flare-ups or diminish their intensity and timing when you gave me a miracle child. I thought if I were faithful and held on through all of this, you would reward me with good or better health. I thought supernatural strength would feel more like physical strength. I thought you would allow me to feel better, or at least not get awful side effects while pregnant so I could just have a moment to enjoy this process. I thought this process of growth wouldn't take so long or feel so very hard. I thought you wouldn't dare allow me to go through a hurricane, while sick as a dog from pregnancy, then start a flare-up, then get another cold with a severe sore throat and have my four year old lose her mind. I thought you would only give me a few things at a time so I could gain my footing a bit more. I didn't think the battle would be this intense for this long. You feel reckless. You feel mean. You feel irresponsible. Don't you see I am drowning here?

    I screamed these accusations while sobbing my eyes out on my bed. I had not been doing the greatest job the last week in guarding my thoughts because honestly, it all felt very true. I felt like I was in way over my head. Completely overwhelmed, drowning, while God held the garden hose over my head. I was sick of reminding myself that these things would pass, and I was blessed, and God was good. I just wanted them to be. I just wanted to be the mom on the playground who was joyful and not so scared and sick. I knew eventually God's promises would come to pass. But I had no clue how I was going to get there in the meantime because I had zero strength left.

The Holy Spirit had been reinforcing throughout the whole week, "You want to become a warrior? This is how we do it. This is how we know strength. This is how we gain ground." I would be in agreement one moment, and face planted in tears the next. I am very sure the surging hormones did very little to help this. But honestly, I wanted to wallow and complain and try to force God's hand into some required miracle. It was the closest I have ever felt to giving up.

But this demon has a name. The dark force of "Enough." It would whisper: "Haven't you been through enough? Haven't you suffered enough? Haven't you been faithful enough? Haven't you held onto trust and your faith for long enough? Is God really enough? This is enough, right?" It took years to be able to call this demon out by name. Thus the rollercoaster would continue. I would hold on for a while, feeling confident in trust and God, and then it would just snap because Enough would get louder and louder. Instead of ordering this voice to be silent, as we have been given the authority to do, I would start agreeing, and thus the collapse. But the moment I understood the sideline ramblings of Enough, I started to gain ground, claimed my power back, and stood firm on my truth that God is the One who strengthens me (Isaiah 51:12 GNT). He will give me the physical and emotional strength I need, as I need it, to sustain me. I will not be left exhausted and depleted. I will be left full, even if all hell breaks out in my life.

So, I am writing this in real-time with brutal honesty, so you can see this process unfold. Literally, as I was weeping on my bed, I asked my husband to grab my computer, so I could start putting these words down. Because I knew if I started writing this all out and I poured out all the vinegar in my heart, I knew I could expect the oil to be there too.

"So Holy Spirit, pour out your truth and oil. Show me what my heart and body need to see and hear. I know you will refill and refresh me. Speak to me, please..."

> *The very first thing I heard was the lyrics to Jenn Johnson's You're Going to Be Ok: "Hold on. Don't let go. Just take one step closer. Put one foot in front of the other. You'll get through this. Just follow the light in the darkness. You're gonna be ok."[14] "I will sustain you. I will uphold you with my righteous right hand" (Isaiah 41:10 NIV). You are near to me. You are loved. I have loved you with an everlasting love. Peace, hope, love: these will cover over everything. Hold on. Go. And a reminder of this lovely passage: "God, my shepherd! I don't need a thing. You have bedded me down in lush meadows; you find me quiet pools to drink from. True to your word, you let me catch my breath and send me in the right direction. Even when the way goes through Death Valley, I'm not afraid when you walk at my side. Your trusty shepherd's crook makes me feel secure. You serve me a six-course dinner right in front of my enemies. You revive my drooping head; my cup brims with blessing. Your beauty and love chase after me every day of my life. I'm back home in the house of God for the rest of my life" Psalm 23 (The Message).*

By the time I finished this chapter, I felt clearer, and my stomach did not hurt as bad. It did not change everything I held in complaint against God, but it did bring me closer to hope.

And that is the rhythm of grace. One step closer. So I say to myself, "This ultimately is just a cold; they pass. I am feeling sick because I am pregnant with a miracle baby. My four year old just needed a nap. This hurricane will be over in twenty-four hours. I have had a billion flare-ups. They suck, they move on. There is nothing here I cannot handle. And I am handling it. This is how I become a warrior, not by surviving the battle, but by looking at the victory. I'm going to be ok."

Girl, there is nothing sacrilegious or arrogant about expecting God to show up and speak. That is faith. I needed God to speak into my darkness and lies right then, and so I expected Him to, and He did. He will do this again and again. And He will do this for you. This is a promise to you. Give Him your battle. This is how we survive: Surrender. It's always surrender.

Warriors, though you may stumble, you will not fall (Psalm 37:24 NIV). You can drown in the anger, or you can "Warrior Up." Take a moment with the Holy Spirit and write out what He is saying to you, and even if you don't feel it, believe it. "Cause when the night is closing in, don't give up and don't give in, it's not the end. You're gonna be ok."[15]

Promises of Strength

What do we do with the days where it all feels like it's a bit too much? Where your nerves are fried, you feel sick, your kids are acting like lunatics, and your husband is all of a sudden incredibly needy or distant. The breathe in and breathe out days, where the anxiety or sadness feels like a cloak, and you have assumed muster position. Reaching for the truth can feel like one more task on your overflowing list, and you just cannot. Tears flow, and you hold up your hands to the Creator and say, "I can't in my own strength. I need yours. I believe you will come through, no matter what the lies are telling me." I have been there, sister. I have lived those many days. I have cried the tears you are crying. Hear me: This will pass. This is but a moment. You are going to be okay, and you are okay. God has not taken a break. He is watching and is wanting you to ask for help. He is just waiting to give you His strength. Claim His promises. And if you can't remember a single one, start here:

- As I continue to follow after God and obey, God will keep me safe, and the evil one cannot touch me. Jesus' hand protects me from the enemy. I am never out of His safety (1 John 5:18).
- I have the mind of Christ (1 Corinthians 2:16).

- As I pray, trust, and praise God, His peace will surpass all of my human understanding and will guard my heart and mind (Philippians 4:7).
- I have the power to overcome fear and the enemy, for the divine that is within me gives me strength and is greater than he who is in the world (1 John 4:4).
- God will provide me with a spirit of wisdom and revelation. He will open the eyes of my heart so I can see Him at work so that I will know the hope to which He has called me (Ephesians 1:17-18).
- God gives me everything I need (Philippians 4:19).
- I can do everything: every hard thing, every difficult thing, everything that tries to break me and cut me down. I can get through it all because Jesus gives me strength (Philippians 4:13).
- I am a masterpiece of God. I have been created by Jesus to do good works that, even before my diagnosis, He has prepared in advance for me to do (Ephesians 2:10).
- I am a warrior. I am more than a conqueror. I am victorious. I win the battles through Him who loves me (Romans 8:37).
- I am filled with the divine and have the power to live a life that is pleasing and good (2 Peter 1:3-4).
- No matter how imperfect I may feel, my body is a temple, a glorious house for the indwelling of the Holy Spirit. He willingly resides and works within me (1 Corinthians 6:19).
- I am precious and honored and deeply loved by God (Isaiah 43:4).
- God will strengthen me with His own power so I may endure everything that comes my way with divine joy (Colossians 1:11).
- Fear is a choice, and I choose to reject it because the Holy Spirit is in me and gives me power, love, and self-control to

control the thoughts of my mind and to release any anxiety or depression (2 Timothy 1:7).

God is saying to you today: "I will fight your battles. All you have to do is stand, believe, and praise. There is never a moment I have forgotten you or your struggle. There has never been a time where my eyes have been off of you. I am working all of this out for your good, for your husband's good, for your family's good. I have this. I will never let you fall. I will pursue your heart to the end of the world. If you let me, I will bring you back stronger and better than you have ever been. I will never leave you empty. I will lead you to peace in every path. I will take care of everything, if you surrender it to Me. I will be constant and never-changing in my love for you. You can pour it all out to me. I can take it. I will never turn my back on you. You are beautiful, chosen, flawless, and enough as you are. My plans for your life are amazing and so full of beautiful moments to take your breath away. Just leave it with me. I want to help you. Please let me fill you with every single thing you need. I will give you strength. With Me, you are so much stronger than you think you are."

Hold on, darling. The warrior in you is being rebuilt—piece by piece. You will be strong, no matter how weak you feel. Remember these promises when the lies are telling you otherwise. Declare your own. Be bold. This moment, day, flare-up, situation will pass. Breathe this moment and the next and let God fill you back up. There is joy coming for you in the morning.

Re-Learning Trust

"You have made your way around this hill country long enough; now turn north" (Deuteronomy 2:3 NIV). It's the exact, perfectly articulated verse to the predicament I was in. My trust and growth had seemed like it had plateaued. And I felt like I kept experiencing the same difficulties over and over again without progress in my response. I would get out of the storm, but it was more by the skin of my teeth or a "How did that happen?" I was battling with my responses to unmet expectations placed on God and my anxiety response based on these disappointments. Why wasn't I further along in my progress? Why was I still battling when I knew the truth? Why was I still going around this hill country time after time after time? I wanted to go North. My soul desperately needed to find North. But as my husband can attest, latitudinal directions are not my thing. I kept claiming every promise I could think of. Saying all the right words, but still struggling.

But often we need a few passes around the mountain before we can find North. Not because North was ever hiding, but simply because we thought we could find it ourselves, and we learn amazing lessons in the hill country. It prepares us for what North has in store. It girds us up and rebuilds what has been broken down.

There is a particular element of self that is needed to assist in the process God is having us walk through, namely, partnership. Doing it all is not our role. God only needed me to say, "I will go where you lead, when you lead, and I will walk through the clearly marked open doors as you open them, but I will not run ahead; and if the pace seems slow, and I feel impatient, that is not because God is slow to bring about His promise of peace and freedom from fear. It is because the process itself is for my good." I was looking at the hill country as the evil, a punishment, an outward manifestation of my lack of spiritual maturity. If I could get it together more, learn better, grow faster, trust stronger, [fill in the blank]. But the hill country is not a consequence. It is a training ground. I realized by trying to outpace God and myself in the hill country, I was not prepared for North.

Months before this revelation, God had given me the most amazing promise: "I will make all your enemies turn their backs and run. I will send the hornet ahead of you to drive [your enemies] out of your way. But I will not drive them out in a single year, because the land would become desolate and the wild animals too numerous for you. Little by little, I will drive them out before you, until you have increased enough to take possession of the land" (Exodus 23:27-30 NIV). God promised to defeat my enemies of anxiety and fear, but not all at once, because I would need the tools to maintain the freedom. If not, I would be overcome the next time anxiety struck because I had not developed the stamina fortified with truth to deal with it. This is the hill country training before the promised land of North.

So it all comes back to trust. Again. I am still in this hill country because God wants me to keep gathering strength and wisdom. What I had failed to grasp was that God is in this hill country, not just in the North. And where He is, is where I am supposed to be. God is walking around with me. He is asking me to stop hating this time; to trust that He knows the best timing to head in a new direction. He wants me to embrace these hills while I am here. It is completely okay to express that sometimes the hills suck and I'm tired. David did that all.the.time. The Psalms are replete with his

Re-learning Trust

groans and complaints. But they always end with his reminders of how God has come through in the past, and He will do it again.

Trust for me, while climbing these hills and valleys, looks like taking a lot of deep breaths and saying, "God, I trust that You know what You are doing and will provide a way out as soon as possible. I am strong enough to handle this until then, and that all the feelings and pains I am experiencing are for my good and God's current best for whatever reason. You will provide for all of my needs, and You love to give good things to Your children. I don't have to understand everything or anything because that is just a desire for control. But I will choose to believe these words, and they will become my truth."

Recommitting to trust is a lifelong journey. It is not a one-shot deal, but rather situational. I learn and re-learn to trust God with every new difficulty that arises. I again have to go back and lay it down. I again have to learn that I am not in control. I again have to stop the worry train and guard my thoughts. I again have to silence the lies that ask: "Will He come through this time, though?" I again have to surrender. I again will have the victory.

God never leaves us empty-handed when we step out in trust. When Job stood the test and did not curse God for all of his misfortunes, devastating losses, and health crises, "The Lord restored [Job's] fortunes and gave him twice as much as he had before" (Job 42:10 NIV). God did this because Job was faithful, and God will not hesitate to absolutely pour out the same blessings on you. This is not a Job-specific thing. This is a God-specific thing. God loves to give good gifts to His kids (Matthew 7:11). He does this because of His nature, not because of how good yours may be. But it all starts again with trust.

You Are Not Sick Girl

I spent years feeling weak and sick. This former Energizer Bunny who could not sit still was learning how to be still for the sake of healing and health. This is a good thing. The problem was more insidious. I did not realize it until three years later, when I began to recognize how I labeled myself and my negative inner monologue. I had come to believe the feelings. I was sick and weak. Not capable. I needed others to care for me. I couldn't trust myself. Unsure and insecure. It was such a moment of clarity.

I had tried my darndest to pinpoint the origin of the anxiety and why it had grown so aggressive so quickly. In retrospect, it is obvious. I had been a respected attorney who felt confident and competent in my field. I was very used to carrying heavy responsibilities and being a rock for everyone else. This is not pride, but the assurance of one's self and position. I felt security. When I became an instant mom, that façade started to drop a bit. Anyone who has become a mother for the first time will be able to relate. You are truly making it up as you go. Never fully feeling prepared but called to draw upon that internal gumption and just do whatever it is you need to do. Being a stay-at-home mother was the most challenging thing I ever did. But SAHMs don't get the street cred we deserve, and we don't see the payoffs until years later, so it's hard to feel as if you are achieving or succeeding. When I started to become sicker within the first eighteen months of my daughter's life, the façade slipped more and more. I felt like I was completely out of control in my life for the first time. Not sure what was happening to me. Still in my career, but transitioning out; and caring for this incredible, crying, needy blessing.

When I was finally diagnosed, the first thing my doctor told me was, "This is going to get worse before it gets better." Not comforting, but he was one hundred percent accurate. I did my first tour of an ER two months later. As mentioned before, I, my husband, our eighteen-month-old child, and eighty-pound dog had to move into my parents' two-bedroom condo so I could get additional daily help, and we hired a nanny. It was humbling, to say the least. With this fun mix of trauma and an untrained mind, it was little wonder the internal monologue started becoming toxic. I felt incapable; therefore, I was. I felt weak; therefore, I was. I felt scared; therefore, I was anxious. I felt sick; therefore, I was simply "sick girl." These lies sank deeper and deeper into my subconscious with every change I had to make to my daily routine. These lies drew their own jagged lines in my neural pathways with every flare-up. I was no longer normal and never would be again. So "sick girl" I was.

Bleak, huh? The anxiety rose the more that "sick girl" played hopscotch in my mind. Because how can you trust "sick girl?" She is too delicate. She can't handle hard emotions. "Sick girl" is scared of her own shadow. "Sick girl" is easily overwhelmed. "Sick girl" is completely self-absorbed. "Sick girl" has lost herself. "Sick girl" is always scared.

I had utterly lost whose I was. I had forgotten how to trust myself and my instincts. I had lost my confidence. And the only thing there to take its place was anxiety. Because "sick girl" is based in a fear dialect, anxiety will fill in the blanks. But no matter how sick I felt on a particular day, I was never "sick girl." "Sick girl" is a lie, and I knew the only way I was going to be able to overcome the anxiety was to put "sick girl" to bed once and for all.

I went to see my pastor to get some spiritual guidance and was explaining this "sick girl" rabbit hole I had dug for myself. She listened patiently, but then said the most poignant words: "I find it remarkable that you look at all that you do while sick and see it as weak because what I have known personally of chronic illness is that is takes tremendous strength to live here." ::Beautiful truth bomb:: Being chronically ill is not easy, and if you are choosing life in this season and you are fighting, then you are a freaking warrior. We all are. How dare I think of myself as weak? How dare I think so little of the person God made me to be. I can continue to look at my victories as trivial because they are not as grandiose as someone's Instagram life, or I can celebrate them and build myself back up.

Girl, if you are like me, we have to change the dialogue. We may feel something, but that does not mean we are that thing. Our identity has nothing, and I mean nothing, to do with our diagnosis. Our truest self is completely separate from this, and never the two shall meet. We must separate the feelings from the truth:

- You feel weak? God says you are strong (2 Corinthians 12:10).
- You see scars and feel ugly? God says you are beautiful and flawless (Song of Solomon 4:7).
- You feel fatigued and tired? God says if you wait on Him, He will renew your strength. You will mount up on wings like eagles. You will run and not grow weary. You will walk and not faint (Isaiah 40:31).
- You feel scared? God says if you follow after Him, you will be secure; you will have no fear; in the end, you will look in triumph on your foes (Psalms 112:7).
- You feel overwhelmed and anxious? God says He will bring you peace and guard your heart and mind (Philippians 4:7).
- You feel used up? God says I have future dreams for you full of hope (Jeremiah 29:11).
- You feel sad? God says He saves those who are crushed in spirit (Psalms 34:18).

- You feel sick? God says He will strengthen you and help you and will uphold you with His righteous right hand."

You are not "sick girl." You are NOT "sick girl!" You Are Not "Sick Girl!" YOU ARE NOT "SICK GIRL!!!" You were made for more. You are so much more. Now repeat.

Section Four
Autumn

The Cure

Often times with chronic illnesses, the med-ical personnel don't have explanations for our multitude of questions. Why did we get this? Where was its origin? How do we stop or slow down its progression? What am I actually diagnosed with?

I spent many years chasing a diagnosis. I needed to know what was happening for my mind to make sense of all this pain. I needed something definitive to hold out and say, "Here, this is the name, and this is the cause." But sadly, I did not really get that. I got a kitchen sink diagnosis with my Central Sensitization Syndrome, but the doctors certainly could not explain why or how to stop it. Pain and symptom management were the only offered solutions. And for someone who feels the need to know why, this was a devastating blow. Because understanding the why makes you feel more in control, as opposed to a freak with a made-up disease.

I did not like the pace at which God was working. It seemed too slow, and I was uncomfortable, so from doctor to doctor and specialist to specialist I went. God knew the ultimate outcome all along, but He also knew I needed to exhaust myself like a tantruming toddler before I was able to calm down and listen.

Our God is a solution-based God. He loves plans and order. The Holy Spirit was sent to us after Jesus was resurrected because God knew we would need a comforter and guide. If you are a Christian, the divine resides in you. He is directing your path. So "Whether you turn to the right or to the left, your ears will hear a voice behind you, saying, 'This is the way; walk in it'"(Isaiah 30:21 NIV). What an amazing gift of a life guru, a guide that will never steer you wrong! Even when we are at a loss for words or feel so overwhelmed, and we have no clue where to start, the Holy Spirit is still working in our favor and is talking to God on our behalf. "In the same way, the Spirit helps us in our weakness. We do not know what we ought to pray for, but the Spirit himself intercedes for us through wordless groans" (Romans 8:26 NIV). So we are never truly at a loss because we have a strong advocate and are filled with divine power. It's not up to you to figure things out on your own. That's just perfectionism or your pride talking. The whole point of being filled with the Holy Spirit is so we are never alone and never have to rely on our own wisdom and strength.

You have been given the mind of Christ (1 Corinthians 2:16). So simply, we have access to the thoughts and wisdom of God Himself. James 1:5 (NIV) states that "if any of you lacks wisdom, you should ask God, who gives generously to all without finding fault, and it will be given to you." God will never hold back His solutions from you. He is not up in heaven scratching his head. He has this already mapped out!

The doctors may not know what you have. They may not even believe you at all. They may never be able to give you a solution. But the Great Physician can. God knows what the best next step is. God knows what we are capable of handling and what our souls need. He is orchestrating a beautiful solution in your life right now—the right doctor, the right medicine, the right modality, the right stress release, the right balance, the right relief. He has it all under His control.

So while you are in the waiting period, tap into your God-given inner strength every moment of every day. There is an unlimited supply. The divine never runs out of power and strength as we do. Believe that God is leading you down the path to the right solution to ease your symptoms or provide a cure. Because He is. He is not looking for us to unjustifiably suffer for kicks and giggles. He knows the rest our minds and bodies need. He will provide a way. Bring Him your problems so He can bless you with the solutions. Praise Him along the way, because "though [the solution may] take time, wait for it; because it will surely come. It won't delay" (Habakkuk 2:3).

You Can Handle This

It does not matter how many times you cried before you could go about your day. It does not matter how many pills you had to take to ease the pain and discomfort. It does not matter how many breakdowns and breakthroughs you had in a day or even an hour. It does not matter how many times you actively had to force yourself from your bed. All that matters is that you are doing it. Is it hard? Of course, it is. Do you wish there was another way? Get in line. But girl, you are doing it.

The simple fact you choose to read this book instead of wallowing means you are doing it. It means you are succeeding. It means you have the moxie of a Joan of Arc in your spirit. You are a badass. You are a warrior, and few can match you for mental and emotional strength. Sickness can break, but not you. You have the divine within you, and you have determined in your heart you will never give up. You will claim the promises of your God. You will see the goodness of your Lord in your lifetime. You are an overcomer. You are more than your illness. You are more than this crappy moment. Girl, hear me well when I say this: You are stronger than those who have never walked in your shoes. I don't care if you can't run a marathon or do CrossFit. That is not the mark of strength and endurance. They chose those obstacles. You did not, and yet you are still enduring. Your very existence sparks hope in so many people without you even knowing it. They hold you as a standard in their minds and say, "If she can do that, I can do this." You are a freaking hero, no matter what the "feelings" say.

On the days where the feelings get too rowdy and they are making you feel worse and less than, guess what? You can handle it on those days too. Tell the feelings and lies to shut up, and go back to the basics. Your God has not changed. You are just feeling overwhelmed today. Overwhelmed is not a fruit of the Spirit. It is a lie. You don't have to believe it. Be kind to yourself, engage in self-care, and tell yourself the truth and then say it again and again because you can handle this and keep on handling this. There has never been a moment in your life when you had to handle this on your own. There has never been a time where God was not willing to offer you grace, strength, mercy, and love. These are all the tools you need. You may want symptom relief. You would be a masochist if you did not. But you do not NEED it. Do you get that? That is just what your mind is telling you. You can handle this, as is. You have been given all that you need. This is in no way advocacy against doctors or throwing away your medicine. God knows He gave you those things as a blessing to help you through difficult times. Take the mercy without guilt or a second thought. God will open the right doors at the right time. Until then, you have it all. You can handle this.

God's promise: "I will not cause pain without allowing something new to be born" (Isaiah 66:9 NIV). Something new is growing inside you. Something beautiful and incredible and worth the wretched wait. You are being reborn and rebuilt. You are okay. You are strong. Your strength comes from above. Stay present with what God is doing right now and do not get wound up in what may happen. God will help you deal with any new thing as it comes up (Matthew 6:34). I'll say it again: You are enough. You have enough. You can handle this.

Condemnation

I was again locked in a spiral. Sitting in my therapist's office, tears running down my face as he spoke the truth I needed to hear: "That is not yours to carry." I had faced this demon before, but to that point had not picked up on its stench. The battle against condemnation was wagging its head again. Now mind you, I never use the word condemnation in my everyday vernacular. Quite frankly, I think Christians may be the only group of people keeping this term alive. I just would blame guilt. But condemnation is deeper and much darker. It's like guilt's older, jerk-off brother with a supersized side of self-loathing.

I had naively thought that if I got pregnant, my husband would be happy. I had erroneously blamed his unhappiness on my illness for years, so maybe, just maybe, if I were able to get pregnant, it would wipe my slate clean in his eyes. So when he did not burst forth in song and joy at the announcement of our miracle, I immediately was shell-shocked. Because he was worried about me and my health with this new baby, I immediately picked up what he was not directly putting down: "If I weren't sick, he would be happy that I was pregnant." ::Condemnation bomb explosion:: I was putting myself in place of God and my husband's own willpower and trying to change something I absolutely could not and had no business trying to change.

I did not cause my illness or try to make it worse in any way. I did not choose this. I have begged God to take it from me, and I have done everything in my power to curtail its effects. So why in the world was I feeling bad, again?

Tell me I'm not alone here? Do you do this too? We go through hell and then feel bad for other people having to watch us go through hell. We tell ourselves that if we were stronger, better, wiser, smarter, less scared, more hopeful, less complaining, more grateful, better Christians, better wives, daughters, friends, mothers or a mother at all, then we would finally be able to get out from under this cloud of guilt we keep letting rain on our head.

But sister, let me just lay down some truth here: God never has and will never put that cloud over your head, and all you have to do is move a step over. We are keeping ourselves under the carefully disguised cloud of condemnation because we feel as if we deserve it. We need to pay some gross penance for some sin we never committed in the first place. But this helps no one. We have never grown stronger or better for remaining in the downpour, and our families and friendships have certainly never benefited from our self-flagellation.

"There is therefore now no condemnation for those who are in Christ Jesus" (Romans 8:1 ESV). God is not condemning us. That is Satan's trick. That is his greatest lie. This is not ours to carry. Self-loathing is not a virtue. It is not the kin of humility. It is the opposite. We need to step outside the rain shower of condemnation and into the freedom of grace and forgiveness. Forgive yourself, drop the bitterness you hold toward those who make you feel as if you deserve the condemnation, and move over.

If you need a helpful practice to bring your mind back every time you try to make it rain again, start by writing out all the weighty things you are carrying that are not from God. All the guilt, the self-loathing, the unmet expectations of others, and even yourself. All the ways you thought your life would go, write it all out, use as many reams of paper as you need. Then burn it, bury it or release it. Whatever feels the best and most environmentally friendly to you, you do it. Don't write it and keep it. Write and free yourself of it. I promise this will be a helpful exercise because when you start to head to the cloud again, you will remember your little practice, and you can turn your back on the rain.

Oh, and by the way, you are not responsible for anyone else's happiness. I do NOT care what the other person is saying or how much shade they are throwing in your direction. I don't care if they are a child or a grown-ass adult. That person is one hundred percent responsible for putting in the hard work of self-growth and actualization, just as you are doing. You are doing them and yourself a great disservice by trying to make them feel as if you can carry this lie for both of you. They will not grow as they need to, and you will enter your cloud, and your growth stops too. It's a lose-lose. Look them in the eye, validate that they have feelings, suggest a good counselor, and then you turn and walk away. You don't own that.

Love yourself as you are right now; God does. Flaws, flare-ups, and all. It is how it should be at this moment. Growth and change take time. God is not angry with any of your perceived lack of progress. He is God. If He wanted an immediate change, then He would just snap His fingers. He is most traditionally a God of process and progress. So let it be. And like the great Elsa has instructed us, "Let it Go."[16]

God's Turn: "If You Only Really Knew"

My Darling Girl, if you only knew how truly loved you are, you would never worry about the future. If you really believed that I saw you and loved you as you were being formed in your mother's womb. That no matter how you were parented, I wanted you. I formed the unique and special you. I love everything about you. It kills my heart when you call things about you "flawed." Do you even know how carefully I crafted you? Do you know that when I look at you, I see remarkable beauty?

Oh Sweet Girl, if you only could see from my eyes, you wouldn't be so scared of this diagnosis, these medications, this doctor's prognosis, this journey. I know that it has rocked your world, but it has not rocked mine. I am still steady, and I will steady you. I have my hands all over this. My love for you is being poured out in even greater measure. I see the tears you are trying to hide from your family. I see the mental and physical struggle. I know every fear scenario you are replaying in your mind about your future. But I know you can handle this. I would never place more on you than I am able to handle for you. I promise to give you everything you need along the way to sustain you. My Spirit will whisper truths to your heart as you sleep to heal your mind and raise you back up. I promise to be faithful and abundant in blessings as you walk through this. Because I am your good Father and you are My beloved child, and I give good and beautiful things to My kids. And not just when you are well-behaved, but simply because I love you.

Daughter, listen to me. I will hold you up. This will not destroy you. This will not destroy your family. I love them too. I am holding them up too. I am sustaining them and giving them what they need. Pour out all the anger and questions. I can handle it. Tell me you don't understand. Tell me this hurts. Tell me you don't know what to do. And I promise I will tell you the truth and show you the right path. I promise to ease your heavy heart and mind. You will not be left with questions and pain. You will be filled instead.

I will walk through this with you. Your hand in My hand. Every doctor's office, every procedure, every new trial of medication, every flare-up, everything. Never will I take My eyes from you. Never will you be completely alone.

I will bring this all about for your good. You will be better off than your wildest dreams. I know that seems like an impossibility right now, but nothing and I mean nothing is impossible for me. You will have freedom in your mind and soul if you keep trusting me.

I know the wait feels so very long. I know you are tired of it. I know you doubt. I don't withhold without a great cause. Can you trust that? Can you trust me? Rest in My arms. Give Me all your burdens. They are not yours to carry. Ease your mind with Me. You will find renewed strength, hope, and peace here. There is only restoration in My story. This life I gave you is not the plotline of struggle; it is a story of victory and peace. You will get there. I will see to it. There is a promised land for you, My Love. Let Me show you the way.

~ Abba

A Year Called Growth

Every year in January, instead of resolutions, I like to ask God to reveal to me a word or phrase for the year. In January of 2019, I was surprised by the response of "Growth." A month prior in December, I was standing before a mountain called a pituitary tumor, and I was in complete shock and fear mode, so the word "Growth" came as such a beacon of hope. There would be more than this. I would move beyond this. But growth does not occur without dramatic change.

The majority of our physical growth occurs in the body when we are young because if it occurred when we were adults, it would hurt like hell. Growth happens in the mind when we take active steps to surrender our thought life to God and turn the negative verbiage into positive, faith-filled affirmations. I will not sugarcoat this for you. Changing years of deeply held lies into life-giving words can feel exhausting, usually because you are trying to do it by yourself instead of inviting the divine in to do the work. But there is no escaping the fact that you have to be so intentional for the first bit of the journey.

And I will also let you in on a not-so-secret. Satan absolutely does not want you to have victory here, so if you feel as if that battle in your thought life all of a sudden starts to heat up intensely in the beginning, make a note that this is not you, this is your enemy wanting to keep you very much down. So congratulations, you are doing something right! Keep going. You may move through different relationships and say goodbye to some. You may change careers or the way you look at the trajectory of your profession. All of this will stretch you. All of this may hurt in the letting go while you are stepping forward to something else. That is normal. Even if the thing you are stepping toward is incredible and to everyone else is the absolute right move, do not allow them to bully your emotions into "what you should be feeling." You must process through even good change.

There is nothing wrong with not liking change; the problem comes in when we try to stop growing because of our discomfort. We cannot be that small-minded and short-sighted. Yes, life is fleeting, but your life will be fuller because of this season of discomfort. God always ends seasons. This discomfort will not last a day longer than it needs to for the sake of your best life.

We all need to go through growth seasons. But they must start with the willing. So what are you asking God for? What kind of faith are you projecting? Because God can do "exceedingly more than we can ask or think" (Ephesians 3:20 NIV). When this year started, I boldly declared, "God, I am done with this fear." I asked God to gird me up. Give me moxie, a warrior spirit. And so we have walked through lots of fear. Together.

God will not withhold growth from you. He loves it. But He will not require it. Let's be honest, growth usually starts with hardship or discomfort, and it can remain there too. That is entirely your decision. Or you can move through it and come out of this season with what you asked for. Don't shy away from these seasons because of fear of pain. That would be the greatest disservice you could do in your life. And as Rachel Hollis reminds us: "embrace the suck."

I never, and I mean never, anticipated what this growth year would truly mean. What an incredibly difficult, challenging, life-altering, amazing year and mountain this has been. It will be the kind of year I will look back on and be so very grateful for. Every time

I think I want to bow out or ask God to put a hold on the process, I am reminded that I am getting what I want. I am becoming free. I am being girded up. I am releasing the fear that has held me back, and all of a sudden, the battle seems worth it again. I put on my big girl armor and know God is fighting these battles with and for me. The enemy does not stand a chance.

Your growth season will inevitably look different than mine, but I hope that you ask for some of the same things. I am learning they are well worth the fight. I wish I could be there when you are on the other side, when you are on top of the mountain, stronger than ever. You are coming up the mountain, my friend. The summit is within reach. Keep climbing.

But How Do I Really?

All of this sounds so good in theory, right? Just trust God. Just cast your cares on Him. Just have faith. Keep hope. All platitudes to the one who is in the ditch struggling. Because how in the world do you actually do this? Everyone would be at peace if it were that easy. I am sure you may have rolled your eyes a few times throughout this book at the lofty thoughts. And maybe even a few of you flipped me the bird and said, "You don't know what I've been through, and you don't know my story." That is true. Everyone is walking out a very different storyline, some with more struggles than others. But I promise you, fellow warrior, that the solutions are still the same.

Taming your thoughts takes time and effort. It will not be a one-and-done deal. It is a learned skill, such as walking. Lots of falling and holding on, but in the end, you will be upright. No one resents her efforts in learning this vital life skill. The problem is we don't value a tamed mind as much as the other growth milestones. We have accepted stress as a valid state of being, and so no one is generally there, ensuring we are taking active steps to overcome this impediment. But it is an impediment, and it must go for proper growth. So do not get sour with the process and efforts. They will result in a life of resilience and peace.

But the real hero in this effort is the Holy Spirit. Because He takes even our marginal efforts and turns them into Olympic-size feats of strength. He bolsters our performance and ensures it lasts.

When we refuse to give the negative thoughts our attention and actively tell God, "I don't want to handle this." Then the peace comes in. But don't for a second again think Satan is going to put his tail between his legs in defeat. The battle to get you to agree with him will continue in sneaky new ways. When this happens, asking God for wisdom to be able to see these attacks clearly and quickly is a great way to get back to the peace you are after.

My girlfriend sent me a message I will never forget. She said, "I was getting discouraged and feeling so beat down, and so I am filling every spare minute I have with praise music or spiritual messages because I need to stay *in the zone*." I used to think that having to stay in the zone was a sign of weakness. Like you can't do this on your own. But how ignorant or really arrogant is that?! Because, guess what, we can't. That is why God created the zone! For our hearts, for our healing, for our protection. The zone is where you find the courage not to fear the unknown, to stop stressing about what is next, to stop worrying about your kids, husband, marriage, job. The zone is where you get to open your hands, and all the things you are holding on to fall into the hands of the One who is capable of handling them.

Listen, you cannot fear or worry your way into any of the solutions you want. I have never changed an outcome by becoming sick to my stomach because I am worried. A tension headache has led me to a solution zero times. The bigger problem is we have bit on the greater lie that if you don't have a negative emotional response to a problem, somehow you must not really care. Bullcrap! Giving that problem over to the One who can actually do something about it, and you staying level-headed and at peace to be able to truly help yourself and family is the absolute most significant thing you can do. No one has ever thanked someone for becoming hysterical in a crisis. Your ability to stay in the zone come hell or high water is your saving grace and a beautiful gift. You don't have to get weird or super religious about this. This does not require time you don't have. You don't have to light a candle and put on special clothes and say particular words. This is a bathroom break with a locked door while you pour out your heart. This is a car ride with praise music as the kids are entertained in the backseat and tears are running down your cheeks. This is taking the break you need to reset and regroup without remorse.

I typically enter the zone by listening to my favorite praise song on repeat and verbally telling God, "You have to take this. I don't want this. I am sick of choosing fear and control over freedom. I'm done. It's yours." This has never failed me. If I need to go back into the zone an hour later because I started worrying again? I do it. What failure is it to you to lay down toxicity? Staying in the zone is how trust is built, and then it becomes easier to enter and have this be your gut reaction as opposed to emotional turmoil.

Sister, let me remind you of this: Jesus could not carry His own cross. We are not meant to carry ours alone, either. Go to the zone as often as you need and leave your burdens there.

The Second Half

I am a big football fan. I was born and raised in New England, so I'll let you make the assumption on my team picks. It's really the only sport I can tolerate in its totality. Soccer is a close second. But there is nothing like football in the fall in New England. I am about to use some sports analogies, so bear with me. I have never seen football played quite like Tom Brady in the second half with two minutes left to play. So many wins and championships have been clinched with what I assumed was way too little time left. But as of the writing of this, six Super Bowl rings cannot be wrong.

The point is this: So often we say, "There is no way this can be turned around. There isn't enough time left for me to start over. I don't have the energy or strength anymore. This is good enough." We limit ourselves, we limit our God, and we settle. But God does not ever work like this. As a matter of fact, God, more often than not, plays the long game. The Bible is so clear that our thinking is often too small. Paul writes of our small minds in Ephesians, where he says God "is able to do exceedingly abundantly above all that we ask or think" (Eph. 3:20 NIV). It is never, ever too late with God.

As I mentioned, I often refer to my sickness as a B.C./A.D. timeline moment. There was before this time, and then there was after this time. But your A.D. life does not have to pale in comparison to your B.C. life! The second to last paragraph of the book of Job starts with this: "The Lord blessed the latter part of Job's life more than the former part" (Job 42:12 NIV). This could be us. This could be our story. We were blessed greater in the second half than the first!

What if we expected more of God simply because we were sick? God didn't allow this sickness and drop the mic. So put it back on Him. "God, if you are allowing this challenge in my life, then I expect You will bless me in the end." Woah, that sounds too presumptuous or arrogant, am I right? We can't require God to bless us. True, we cannot tell God *how* to bless us. But if He is allowing the fire and you are holding on, even by the skin of your teeth (remember all you need is faith the size of a mustard seed), then God, true to His character, *will* bless you with a life far greater than you could have ever thought. This is no guarantee on a hiatus of bad things happening or a mansion. There are no pain quotas in life. But if you begin to see things through His eyes instead of your narrow, self-focused perception, then you will realize, this second half is far greater than the first.

Of course, I don't want to be sick, but while sick and holding on to my mustard seed, God started to rebuild my marriage. While sick, God provided the avenue to enter a less stressful career where I can create beauty and focus on the things that matter. While sick, I was able to conceive a miracle baby. While sick, God provided for all of my needs and exceeded my expectations. While sick, I wrote this book. I had always wanted these things, but the B.C. path was not leading me to them.

You don't have to fear this second half because it is filled with so much promise of hope and goodness. You don't have to see this as the end. Because it absolutely is not, and if you are faithful, God promises it will not be the end. You will see the goodness of your God in your lifetime (Psalm 27:13). God will restore the years the locusts have destroyed (Joel 2:25). This is your greatest half. This is your time to thrive and shine. The second half is your best life!

The Second Half

Topple over the pedestal you are still putting the first half of life on. Take down the altar. It is not helping you when keep looking backward. That life may have been good or even great. You may long for the freedom you felt in your body in those days. And you need to properly allow your body to go through the stages of grief. It's natural and healthy. But there is more freedom to come. There are greater adventures, learning, and growth to come. Enter your second half expecting great things, and have outrageous hope. You will not be disappointed. You are Tom Brady with two minutes left (sorry I couldn't help it).

Even Better Than Before

This story of the Israelite Nation picks up after they had been led away as slaves to the mighty nation of Babylon. But God moved within the heart of the conquering king, and he allowed a small group of people to leave captivity and go back to their land and rebuild the temple of God that had been destroyed. Now mind you, the original temple had been a wonder of the world. Dignitaries from all over the known world were aware of Solomon's temple and would travel months to see its splendor. Walls with precious stones and gold floors and the finest linens and craftsmanship were just a few of its boasts. These slaves on furlough had nothing close to this in hand to start to rebuild. The people were feeling the pressure. They were sitting ducks in a broken land with a momentous task in front of them.

Then God speaks to a man named Haggai, and this is what He instructs Haggai to tell this ragtag group: "Ask them, 'Who of you is left who saw this house in its former glory? How does it look to you now? Does it not seem to you like nothing?'" (Haggai 2:3 NIV). A harsh introduction to what the people can already see with their eyes. They remembered the glory of yesteryear. They longed for the way life used to be. They wanted things to go back to normal. They knew how great it was before and how little they had in their hands now. But God was not finished with His speech: "'Be strong, all you people of the land,' declares the Lord, 'and work. For I am with you,' declares the Lord Almighty. 'This is what I covenanted with you when you came out of Egypt. And my Spirit remains among you. Do not fear'" (Haggai 2:4-5 NIV). God is not just going to drop gold and precious stones down from heaven. He is not going to send His Angel Armies to rebuild the temple for them. He will require that they work. But they do not need to fear while the rebuilding process occurs, because His love and promises have not changed.

God finishes up His decree with this in Haggai 2:9 (The Message): "This Temple is going to end up far better than it started out, a glorious beginning but an even more glorious finish." "And in this place, I will grant peace" (Haggai 2:9 NIV). For all intents and purposes, this rebuilt temple never held the aesthetic glory of its earlier version. But the glory and peace of God rested deeper and fuller in this place than Solomon's temple ever dreamed.

You see where I am going with this? There are times in our lives when we go through something earth-shaking and shattering, and the frame of who we have built ourselves to be comes crashing down, and all we are left with is ruins. This disease or chronic condition has been this moment for many of us, a full reset to our previous lives. And standing in the rubble is overwhelming. The memories of how everything used to be have become haunting, not reassuring. You don't know how you will get back to that. How do you rebuild this?

You don't. At least not on your own. God most likely will not send His Angel Armies to transform you overnight, but with work and God's help and a handful of promises backing you every step of the way, you will be rebuilt. It may not look anything close to what "before" was for you. Do not get hung up on that. It will be better. And God's peace will rest on you. Here is God's promise: "I have loved you with an everlasting love; I have drawn you with loving-kindness. I will build you up again, and YOU WILL BE REBUILT" (Jeremiah 31:3-4 NIV).

Even Better Than Before

You may come away with a few scars. I have the scar of my thyroidectomy to daily remind me of this journey. A permanent manifestation of where I have been. And even though the rebuilding process has lead me to a life I never imagined, it is better and fuller and more peaceful than it has ever been. Darling, let God rebuild you. Don't fight him. Don't let the past win. Not now, after all you have been through. Love your new temple. Embrace its new majesty. It is better, now believe that.

At Least Remember This

I see in retrospect how God was girding up my soul to stand up against what was about to be blasted in my face. God constantly replayed in my mind, "But now, this is what the LORD says— he who created you, he who formed you: Do not fear, for I have redeemed you; I have summoned you by name; you are mine" (Isaiah 43:1 NIV). This is the graciousness of God, and so many times I have looked back and seen the hand of God when I could never have seen it at that present moment. Hindsight is, as they say, truly 20/20. I never thought that by writing this book I would be the one wholly changed. Or how many times it saved me. The times I did not want to write or did not know what to write, but then the words started pouring out, and my heart was healed a bit more. The times I would go back and reread a section because I needed to be reminded of the truth, and the fear would wash away. The times where I doubted or wanted to give up, but I knew deep down, I did not come up with these words and concepts on my own. God gave me these messages, and I would believe again.

    This life is a journey, healthy or not. No one is escaping that. Growth is a lifelong process, and may we always be learners. If I can leave you with one message, it would be this: This is your second half of life. No more comparisons. This is a new beginning. A beautiful one. Fuller of promise and hope than ever. God will show up in ways that will leave you breathless and in awe if you keep believing. Reject all the lies, no matter how true they feel.

You can do this. Keep your head up. You are a warrior. You are so very loved. You are never alone. You are enough. You are going to get through this. Find your tribe. Hold on. Never, ever, ever give up hope. This is how you fight your battles: Surrender to the One who always wins. Peace is a possibility, but only if you cast off all the things you cannot carry on our own. God will do this. You will win. Because what once hindered you, is only a part of this beautiful story you will get to tell. I hope I get to hear it. Go find your peace, Warrior Friend. You know the way.

References

[1] Fairweather, D., & Rose, N. R. (2004). Women and Autoimmune Diseases. *Emerging Infectious Diseases*, *10* (11), 2005-2011. https://dx.doi.org/10.3201/eid1011.040367.

[2] River, Jonas. Docter, Peter. "Up." 2009. United States: Walt Disney Picture and Pixar Animation.

[3] Brown, Brene, *Braving the Wilderness: The Quest for True Belonging and the Courage to Stand Alone*, Random House, New York, 2017.

[4] Neiquist, Shauna, *Present Over Perfect: Leaving Behind Frantic for a Simpler, More Soulful Way of Living*, Zondervan, California, August 9, 2016.

[5] https://www.eclecticenergies.com/enneagram/type3. Copyright Ewald Berkers. 2003 to 2019

[6] Gretzinger, Steffany. "Pieces: Spontaneous" Have It All. Bethel Music. 2016. Track 6.

[7] Saujani, Reshman. *Brave, Not Perfect: Fear Less, Fail More, and Live Bolder*, Penguin Random House, Westminster, London, England,2019.

[8] Metro Goldwyn Mayer; Act III Communications; directed by Rob Reiner; screenplay by William Goldman; produced by Andrew Scheinman and Rob Reiner. "The Princess Bride." Santa Monica, CA: MGM Home Entertainment, 1987.

[9] Rohr, Richard. *Falling Upward: A Spirituality for the Two Halves of Life*, First Edition, *San* Francisco, California, Jossey-Bass, 2011.

[10] Ibid.

[11] Ten Boom, Corrie., John L Sherrill, and Elizabeth Sherrill, *The Hiding Place*, Barbour, Westwood, New Jersey, 1971.

[12] Brown, Brene. "Joy: It's Terrifying." SuperSoul Sunday. Oprah Winfrey Network. Mar 17, 2013.

[13] Your menstrual cycle, for those who don't use this vernacular.

[14] Johnson, Brian and Jenn. "You're Gonna Be Ok." After All These Years. Jason Ingram, Paul Mabury. 2017. Track 9.

[15] Ibid.

[16] Walt Disney Animation Studios; directed by Chris Buck, Jennifer Lee; produced by Peter Del Vecho; screenplay by Jennifer Lee; story by Chris Buck, Jennifer Lee, Shane Morris. "Frozen." Burbank, California. Walt Disney Pictures. 2013.

CPSIA information can be obtained
at www.ICGtesting.com
Printed in the USA
BVHW030954060420
576973BV00001B/58